A
DICTIONARY
OF
TOPONYMS

A
DICTIONARY
OF
TOPONYMS

Nigel Viney

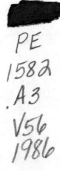

LA

THE LIBRARY ASSOCIATION · LONDON

Published by
Library Association Publishing Ltd
7 Ridgmount Street
London WC1E 7AE

First published 1986

British Library Cataloguing in Publication Data

Viney, Nigel
    A dictionary of toponyms.
    1. Gazetteers   2. Toponymy
    I. Title
    910.014   G103.5
    ISBN 0-85365-747-5

Typeset in 11/12 point Baskerville by Allset Composition, London.
Printed and bound in England by Redwood Burn Limited,
Trowbridge, Wilts

Contents

Introduction

Toponyms are place-names which have come to mean something more than the name of a place. This compilation seeks to list, and elucidate where necessary, the most common English-language toponyms which a reader might expect to encounter.

Toponyms fall into three main categories. Some derive from a place-name without this being immediately apparent: such words as *sherry, spruce, sisal* and *satin* are examples. Then there are words which clearly come from a place-name, but not always for obvious reasons: *canary, canterbury* and *china,* for instance. Lastly there are two-word toponyms, such as *French polish, Dutch courage* and *German measles.*

Some categories of words have such an abundance of toponyms that, if they had been included, they would have overwhelmed the book. As a consequence, breeds of dog, breeds of domestic fowl, cheeses and wines have been almost entirely omitted.

Throughout the book, listed toponyms are printed in italics. Toponyms from fiction are indicated by (F). Spurious toponyms: words which sound as though they have been derived from a place-name but in fact have not, are indicated by (S).

Acknowledgements

This dictionary has grown, so to speak, from *Magenta Marathon Mecca*, a short glossary of toponyms published in 1984 by Abson Books.

As is to be expected, many works of reference have proved most valuable, including *Hobson-Jobson*, several of Eric Partridge's books, Cunnington's *Dictionary of English costume* and the indispensable, majestic *Oxford English Dictionary*.

I am greatly indebted to friends and correspondents for suggestions and help, including Barley Alison, Betty Arne, Frank Atkinson, Jean and Tony Bagnall-Smith, John Blackwell, Charles Boycott, Rosie Boycott, Jim Cochrane, C. T. Codrington, Carmelle Denning, Roland Gant, Douglas Graham, Neil Grant, Al Haman, Stephen Hirschberg, Laurence Knighton, David Merriam, George Mikes, Olga Norris, Geoffrey Powell, Tom Rosenthal, Roger Smith, Madelaine Smout and Joan Wolfenden.

I would be glad to receive suggestions for additions and corrections in future editions.

Nigel Viney

Dedicated to
a valley in France, a village in Suffolk
(or a county in Ireland), a river in Massachussetts,
a bay in Galloway, and a village on the
Dornoch Firth

A

Abbotsford   Victorian-Jacobean carved oak furniture is known as *Abbotsford*, from the name of Sir Walter Scott's home. Scott (1771-1832) had built his gabled and turretted house below the Eildon Hills in 1812, and filled it with antiquities and relics of the past. Illustrated works such as Joseph Nash's *Mansions of England* had familiarized the public with the appearance of the house, inside and out. The immensely popular best-selling author's study and library may be said to have given the name of *Abbotsford* to a whole style of furniture.

Aberdeen   The city of *Aberdeen* has given its name to *Aberdeen fish-hooks*, as well as to *Aberdeen terriers*, often called *Scotch terriers*. With the neighbouring former county of *Angus*, the name is also used for the famous *Aberdeen Angus* beef cattle. The breed was developed in the district in the nineteenth century. The black, hornless cattle were first taken to America in 1873, rapidly replacing there the long-horn as the prime beef cattle.

Academia   It was in the olive-grove of *Academia*, outside Athens, that Plato (ca 429-347 BC) founded his *Academy*. The word went on to mean the philosophical school, or system of Plato. Later it came to mean any school or institution for the study of arts or science, or training for a particular skill. Spelt *achadomye* it was used in one of Caxton's books, dated 1474.

Achetes, River   *Agates* are named after the river *Achetes* in Sicily, in which district the precious stones were once found. *Agates* are striped, or clouded, or can have irregular markings, some of which resemble foliage; lapidaries distinguish these as *moss agates*.

Acol   Many of the best bridge players use the *Acol* system of bidding. The name comes from the former *Acol Club*, in *Acol Road*, Hampstead, London, where it was developed; the system first attracted attention in 1937.

1

Afghanistan The knitted wool coverlets called *Afghans* take their name from their original country of origin. *Afghan hounds* also take their name from *Afghanistan*. *Afghans* are a very ancient breed and, although they were not shown in Britain until 1907, rock carvings showing dogs of this type have been dated 2200 BC.

Albany In the nineteenth century sturgeon were sometimes called *Albany beef*. The reason for this was that sturgeon, some weighing as much as 200 lb, could be taken from the Hudson River at *Albany*, the State Capital of *New York* State.

Alderney Many breeds of cattle are named after counties or districts; none is as small as the island of *Alderney*, one of the three Channel Islands to have given their names to breeds of cattle.

Alps An *Alpine jacket*, said to be an improved form of the *Norfolk jacket*, was introduced in the 1870s.

America *American cloth*, waterproof enamalled oilcloth once much used for tablecloths in pre-plastic days, was strangely named, as it was a nineteenth-century British invention, perhaps called *American* for promotional purposes. *American shoulders*, known to tailors, are named after the broad, straight, padded shoulders which were once worn by male *American* tourists in Europe; the phrase dated from 1875.

Angora In 1923 Kemal Atatürk (1881-1938) moved the capital of *Turkey* from Constantinople to *Angora*, now known as *Ankara*. *Angora* had already given its name to *Angora cats*, *Angora rabbits* and *Angora goats*, whence comes the silky and hairy *Angora wool*.

Angostura The proprietary name *Angostura bitters* comes from Venezuela. The *bitters* is made from tree bark (*Galipea* or *Cusparia febrifuga*) growing near *Angostura* or *Angustura*. The place, on the Orinoco River, was renamed Ciudad Bolivar in 1846. *Angostura bitters* was first made there in 1824, but production of the celebrated flavouring was later moved to
2

Port-of-Spain, Trinidad. *Angostura bitters* is much used in cocktails, and in gin-and-bitters or 'pink gin', once the favourite drink of the wardrooms of the Royal Navy.

Apollinarisburg *Apollinaris water,* sometimes shortened to *polly',* is a proprietary effervescent mineral water introduced to Britain about 1870. It takes its name from *Apollinarisburg,* where it was first produced. *Apollinarisburg* is near Remagen, on the Rhine between Bonn and Koblenz.

Arabia The spirited, intelligent, strong and agile *Arab* breed of horses was first known in about 400 BC. All Thoroughbred horses, the English breed developed for speed, trace their descent from one of three imported *Arab* stallions: the *Byerley Turk* (1689), the *Darley Arab* (1700) and the *Godolphin Barb* (1724).

Arauco The monkey-puzzle tree (*Araucaria imbricata*) gets its Latin name from the province of *Arauco,* Chile. It has been cultivated as an ornamental tree in Britain since about 1830.

Arkansas There is a species of Bowie knife, in which the blade can be depressed into the handle, known as an *Arkansas toothpick.*

Armagnac The district of *Armagnac* is part of Gascony and lies in the *département* of Gers, to the west of Toulouse. Many consider the brandy made there to be superior to that made in the other famous brandy-producing district of France, *Cognac.* In both places it is customary to distil the wine in the winter after fermentation.

Armenia *Armenian cloaks* and *Armenian mantles* were fashionable wear for men in the 1850s and 1860s. Ample, sleeveless garments, they were so called from their resemblance to those worn in *Armenia.* Embroiderers are familiar with pretty edges called *Armenian edges.*

Arras *Arras* today is the chief town of the *département* of Pas-de-Calais. Of strategic importance in World War I, a battle was fought there on 9 May 1915. In former times it was a

3

famous centre for the making of tapestries and other hangings. As 'hoover' has come to mean vacuum-cleaner, *arras* came to mean any tapestry or hanging, wherever made. *Hamlet* III. iv has several stage directions about the *arras*, which Polonius hides behind, with a fatal result. There was also *Arras lace*.

Artois *Artesian* wells were first made, in the eighteenth century, in the old province of *Artois*, in northern *France*. In this ingenious type of well, the water rises to ground level by its own pressure. Such wells can only be located in the central area of saucer-shaped geological formations. The well punctures the permeable rock in which the water lies, and the pressure of the surrounding geological formation causes the water to come to the surface. *Artois buckles*, very large shoe-buckles for men, were briefly fashionable in the late eighteenth century.

Ascot Not far from *Windsor* is the royal race-course of *Ascot*, where the fashionable *Ascot Week* occurs each June, always a 'dressy' occasion. Formal wear for men can include the wearing, instead of a necktie, of a stock or *cravat*. In *America* these are known as *ascots*, puff-scarves, *ascot ties* or *puffed ascots*.

Asti A popular substitute for *champagne, Asti Spumante* 'foaming wine of *Asti*', comes from the town of *Asti*, in Piedmont, north *Italy*.

Astrakhan True *astrakhan* is the skin, with its fur-like wool, of still-born or very young lambs from the Russian province of *Astrakhan*, on the lower Volga, adjacent to the Caspian sea. It was especially popular for collars and hats from the eighteenth century.

Atlas The *Atlas cedar (Cedrus atlantica)* was introduced to Britain in 1845, from its native habitat in the *Atlas* mountains of Algeria and *Morocco*.

Attica/Athens Now more than often called 'roof-space' an *attic* lies between the ceiling of the top storey of a house and a pitched roof and is normally approached by a ladder. Literally, *attic* means Athenian. The *Attic* order of archi-
4

tecture is a decorative structure, consisting of a small order placed above another order of much greater height, constituting the main facade. The first recorded user of the word in its modern sense is Daniel Defoe, writing in 1724. *Attic wit*, also Athenian is defined as delicate and refined.

Austria Heavy black silk braid ornamentation appliquéd in looped designs first appeared on *Austrian* uniforms of the eighteenth century. Known as *Austrian knots*, they were copied by Napoleonic and all other military forces.

Axminster An *Axminster* carpet is of a seemless type originally made at *Axminster*, and noted for its thick and soft pile, resembling that of a *Turkey* carpet. Carpet manufacture was started at *Axminster* in *Devonshire* in 1755, came to an end 80 years later, and restarted there in 1937.

Ayrshire The *Ayrshire* breed of cattle is one of the many breeds which were established in the nineteenth century.

B

Babylon   Genesis 11 describes the construction of a city and a tower at *Babel*, and the ensuing confusion of languages. *Babel* is a rendering in English of the Hebrew word for *Babylon*, the capital city of the Chaldean empire. *Babble* developed from *Babel*. *Babylon* can be used to describe any large and luxury-loving city, as Arnold Bennet did in *The Grand Babylon Hotel*.

Badminton   A character in Disraeli's *Lothair* refers to being 'soothed or stimulated by fragrant cheroots and beakers of *Badminton*'. *Badminton* is a drink made from claret, sugar and soda-water, which took its name from *Badminton* House, the seat of the Dukes of Beaufort in *Gloucestershire*. Later, on a wet weekend in the 1870s, the indoor game of *Badminton* was invented, using rackets and shuttlecocks from the ducal nursery. From this casual beginning, the game has spread across the world, being especially popular in the Far East.

Baghdad   The Italian word for the city of *Baghdad* is *Baldacco*. In medieval times, *Baghdad* produced and exported a rich fabric much used for canopies, especially in churches, which thus became known as *baldachin, baldaquin* or *baldacchino*. The word went on to be used for permanent architectural canopies of stone or metal, often above altars in churches and cathedrals.

Bakewell   *Bakewell tart* is pastry lined with a layer of jam and filled with a rich almond paste, and baked. The name comes from the town of *Bakewell*, in *Derbyshire*. Authorities in the town, however, say that the correct name for the dish is *Bakewell pudding*, which came to be made through a misunderstanding at the Rutland Arms Inn in the mid-nineteenth century; *Bakewell pudding* is made in the town to this day.

Balaklava   A *balaclava* helmet is a knitted woollen covering for head and shoulders. It was much worn on active service, and by explorers and mountaineers in the late nineteenth and early twentieth centuries. Like cardigan and raglan (both named after Generals) *balaclava* is a word from the Crimean

6

War, from the Battle of *Balaklava*, fought on 25 October 1854. Study of photographs suggests that *balaclavas* were not actually worn at the time; they seem to have been invented somewhat later, and got their name from the thought that they would have been useful and popular during the appalling Crimean winters. It was bearded soldiers returning from the Crimea who made beards popular and fashionable in Victorian Britain, and these too were for a time known as *balaclavas*.

Balmoral   *Balmoral cloth* is a twill weave striped in red, grey, blue or black. *Balmoral boots* are high-uppered shoes or half-boots laced in front. A *Balmoral petticoat* is a red woollen underskirt striped in black and worn under a looped-up skirt for walking. There are also *Balmoral cloaks, Balmoral jackets* and *Balmoral mantles*. A *Balmoral* is a round flat cap with an all-round projecting top. All these came into use after the royal family had bought the *Balmoral* estate in Aberdeenshire in 1848. The last is still in use, as the *Balmoral* is worn by some Highland Regiments, such as The Black Watch.

Banbury   *Banbury cakes* came from the Oxfordshire market-town; they are small puff-pastry cakes with mincemeat filling.

Bangalore   A *Bangalore torpedo* is a military device, a long metal pipe filled with explosive, used for clearing barbed-wire entanglements and for other purposes. It was mentioned in an Army manual dated 1913, and is believed to have been invented by a military engineer at *Bangalore*, the principal army station in Mysore from early in the nineteenth century.

Bantam   *Bantams* are a small variety of domestic fowl *(Gallus bankiva)*. They take their name from the place where they were first seen by Europeans. This was *Bantam* (now *Banten*), a town in west Java, some 50 miles west of Jakarta (formerly Batavia). The Dutch East India Company formed a settlement there in 1602, and found this local breed of small domesticated chickens. The word has gone on to mean anything undersized. In professional boxing, *bantamweight* means 8 st to 8 st 6 lb. In World War I the British Army formed *Bantam* battalions from men who were below the official height limit. The 35th Division was a *Bantam Division*.

Barbizon The *Barbizon School* was a mid-nineteenth century coterie of French painters. Partly inspired by English landscape painters, especially John Constable (1776-1837) and linked by friendship and poverty, they established themselves, about 1830, in the village of *Barbizon*, near Fontainebleau. Théodore Rousseau (1812-67) was their leader. The *Barbizon School* introduced the British public to naturalism, which led to the rediscovery of Constable.

Barcelona *Barcelona handkerchiefs* were popular in the eighteenth and nineteenth centuries; they were of soft twilled silk and usually black.

Barracks In the 1880s noisy games of football were played on waste ground near *Victoria Barracks*, Melbourne. It is quite probably from there that the term *barracking* to denote derisive shouting evolved. On the other hand, the word may have come from the aboriginal word *borak* (banter). In any event, the word certainly has an Australian origin, something which causes no surprise, since attempts of this kind to disconcert a player, or performer, or speaker frequently seem natural to Australians.

Bath The City of *Bath* took its name from the Roman *baths* there. The place was a resort from Roman times, when it was called Aquae Sulis ('waters of Sul') from a shadowy local deity. Over the centuries, the city has given its name to many things. *Bath stone* and *Bath brick* were much used for the buildings of the city. *Bath chairs* were invented for the invalids who flocked to *Bath* in search of health. Pigs' cheeks are called *Bath chaps* by butchers. *Bath buns* are well known. *Bath Oliver biscuits* were invented and promoted by a noted eighteenth century *Bath* physician, Doctor William Oliver, as part of the cure for obesity developed at the Royal Mineral Water Hospital.

Battenberg The *Battenberg jacket*, an outdoor jacket for women with loose front, large buttons and a turn-down collar, became fashionable soon after Princess Victoria of *Hesse*, a grand-daughter of Queen Victoria, had married Prince Louis of *Battenberg* in 1884. The British branch of the *Battenberg* family changed its name to Mountbatten in 1917. *Battenberg cake*, made in multi-coloured squares and covered in marzipan, is still popular today.

8

Baux, Les *Bauxite*, the chief source for the production of aluminium, is an earthy compound of aluminium oxide, titanic acid, iron oxide and water. It is to be found in southern *France*, Guyana, Northern Ireland and North America. It takes its name from *Les Baux*, in Provence, between Arles and Avignon. When first dug there, in 1847, the place was known as *Les Beaux*, and the product as *Beauxite*.

Bayonne Originally *bayonet* referred to a short, flat dagger. By the eighteenth century, however, the word had come to mean a steel stabbing implement which could be fixed to a musket (and later to a rifle). It was the development of the *bayonet* which led to the demise of the pike as an infantry weapon. The word comes from the city of *Bayonne* in south-west *France*, where *bayonets* were first made. The word was also used as a measure of military strength: Mussolini often boasted 'Eight million *bayonets* guard *Italy*'. There is also a *Bayonne* ham.

Béarn *Béarnaise sauce* (chopped fresh herbs cooked with shallots in white wine and thickened with egg yolk) takes its name from the former French province of *Béarn*, once the most southerly English possession and now part of the *département* of Pyrénées-Atlantiques. It barely qualifies as a toponym, because it is so named because the sauce was invented at a *Paris* restaurant called 'Henry IV' in the early nineteenth century. This monarch, the first of the *Bourbon* line, came from *Béarn*, and was known as 'Le Grand *Béarnais*'.

Bedford/Bedfordshire *Bedford cord* is hard-wearing twill with prominent cords running in the direction of the warp. Much used for riding breeches, it was originally made in the town of *Bedford*. The pun 'up the stairs to *Bedfordshire*' has been used by countless generations of parents urging their children to bed; it first appeared in print in 1665.

Beijing The Chinese capital, now usually transliterated as *Beijing*, used to be spelt *Pekin(g)* by Europeans. During this time it gave its name to *Pekin man*, a type of prehistoric man whose remains were found there; to *pekin*, a silk material; and to the long-haired *Pekingese* lap-dogs.

Bengal In Hindi, *bangla* means 'of *Bengal*'. *Bungalow* means 'a house built in *Bengal* style'. This meant, in *India*, a single-storey house with a pitched roof and a verandah. In Britain and *America* today, *bungalow* means any single-storey dwelling. Until *India* and Pakistan became independent in 1947, much of the British professional soldier's time was spent in the Indian sub-continent. As a consequence, much Army slang came from *India*; *Bengal blanket* was army slang for the sun.

Benghazi A *Benghazi cooker* is an army contrivance, an extemporized cooking-stove made from a petrol-can, filled with petrol-soaked sand. It was named after the Libyan seaport which featured in the desert fighting in 1940-42.

Bergen A *bergen* is a type of metal-framed rucksack, much used in the armed forces and first developed at *Bergen*, the second largest city of *Norway*, in the 1930s. Neither rucksack nor knapsack are toponyms, although there is a German town of Knapsack.

Berkshire The *Berkshire* breed of pigs is the first of the British pig breeds to have been improved, by care, attention and the keeping of records, which date back to 1850.

Berlin A *berlin*, sometimes spelt in the French manner *berline*, was a popular and fashionable type of four-wheeled covered carriage (Chesterfield, writing from *Bath* in 1746, commiserates with his son about his 'broken *berline*'). They were introduced by an officer of The Elector of *Brandenburg* about 1670, and take their name from the city of *Berlin*. *Berlin wool* is fine, dyed wool used for tapestry, knitting etc; *Berlin work* is cross-stitch worked on squared canvas in such wool — something which has been popular since the 1830s. *Berlin gloves* (strong cotton gloves for men) have been known as such since 1830 or thereabouts.

Bermuda Gaffless tapering sails are the mark of a *bermuda*-rigged vessel; the style has been in use since the middle of the nineteenth century. The lengthy *Bermuda shorts*, or *bermudas* were also invented in the islands about a century later — the earliest reference in the *Oxford English Dictionary* is from a Raymond Chandler novel of 1953. The name for these

10

garments is better than the army term for similarly lengthy tropical shorts, which bore the deliciously absurd official name of 'shorts, long'. In the first half of the eighteenth century there were *Bermuda hats*, straw hats for women's country wear.

Bethlehem   *Bedlam* (chaos, uproar, confusion) is a corruption of *Bethlehem*. It all began with the founding, by Simon Fitzmary, of a priory in Bishopsgate, in the City of *London*, under St Mary's of *Bethlehem*. It was later converted to a madhouse; and then, in 1676, moved to Moorfields. In 1815 it moved again to *Lambeth*, and finally, in 1931, to Beckenham, in Kent. The building *Bedlam* occupied in *Lambeth* is now part of the Imperial War Museum.

Bewdley   *Bewdley caps* were similar to *Monmouth caps*, and originated at *Bewdley, Worcestershire*. The caps remained popular with country people until the nineteenth century.

Bikini Atoll   In July 1946 *Bikini Atoll*, in the Marshall Islands was used by the American authorities for atomic bomb tests. The name was then used for skimpy, strapless two-piece swim-suits which first appeared on French beaches in 1947, their design being attributed to an engineer, Louis Reard (1897-1984). In fact the garment was hardly practical, as few figures could maintain the top half of the garment in position satisfactorily. Shoulder-straps were re-introduced, but the name *bikini* was kept, and is now used for any two-piece female swimsuit. *Monokini*, which wittily designates the bottom half of a *bikini* worn on its own, came into use in 1964.

Bilbao   A *bilbo* was a rapier or sword with a finely-tempered blade. They were originally made at *Bilbao*, northern *Spain*, much noted for its iron and steel, and long known in Britain as *Bilboa*. Falstaff uses the word, in this sense, in *The Merry Wives of Windsor*, III. v. *Bilboes*, similarly derived from *Bilbao*, were also long iron bars with sliding shackels used for confining sailors in irons; some of these, taken from ships which sailed in the Spanish Armada of 1588, are to be seen in the Tower of London.

11

Billingsgate   To talk *billingsgate* is to use foul or abusive language. The expression comes from the alleged verbal habits of the porters and fishwives in *Billingsgate Fish Market*, formerly in the City of *London*, and now removed to West India Dock, in the borough of Tower Hamlets, but still under the authority of the City.

Blarney   *Blarney* is smoothly flattering speech of dubious veracity. It comes from the village of *Blarney*, near Cork in southern Ireland. The name is applied because of a legend dating from the year 1602, when a certain Cormac Macarthy undertook to surrender *Blarney* castle to the English as part of an armistice agreement. Every day, the Lord President Carew looked for fulfilment of the terms of the armistice, but all he got was soft speeches, until he became the laughing stock of the land. An additional, and more improbable legend, has it that anyone succeeding in kissing the awkwardly-placed *Blarney* stone, in the castle, acquires Cormac Macarthy's gift of the gab.

Blenheim   The famous *Blenheim pippin* or *Blenheim orange*, a golden-coloured apple was first grown, in the 1870s, at *Blenheim Palace*, Woodstock in Oxfordshire, the seat of the Dukes of Marlborough, a place which also gave its name to the *Blenheim spaniel*, a kind of King Charles Spaniel with red and white markings. The Palace is named after the great victory of the first Duke of Marlborough (1650-1722) at *Blenheim*, in Bavaria.

Bloomsbury   *The Bloomsbury Group* is defined as 'a "school" of writers and aesthetes living in or associated with the *Bloomsbury* district of London'. Gordon Square was the heart of the *Group*, which began to emerge during 1910, centred around the two daughters of Sir Leslie Stephen (1832-1904), Virginia (1882-1941) and Vanessa (1879-1961), and included their husbands Leonard Woolf (1880-1969) and Clive Bell (1881-1964) as well as their friends Lytton Strachey (1880-1932), E. M. Forster (1879-1970), Roger Fry (1866-1934), Duncan Grant (1885-1978), J. M. Keynes (1883-1946) and G. E. Moore (1873-1958). Supposed 'members' of the *Group* were sometimes called *Bloomsberries*.

12

Bohemia   As *gipsies* were supposed, in Britain, to have come from *Egypt*, they were popularly supposed in *France,* when they first arrived in the fifteenth century, to have come from the Kingdom of *Bohemia*, then part of the *Austrian* empire. Later the meaning was transferred to gipsies of society — artists or writers leading a vagabond life.

Bologna   A *Bologna* sausage is made from a variety of meats, smoked and seasoned; it takes its name from the north Italian city of *Bologna*. The claim that they were invented there was first made in print in 1596. In *America*, the word is sometimes spelt as it is pronounced *Boloney*. If the sausage is the origin of the other meaning of this word (balderdash) it is because a sausage consists of chopped up meat stuffed into a casing, while *boloney* can be said to be a story which is mixed up and stuffed into the hearer's ears. This seems more far-fetched than the other possible derivation of *boloney*, synonymous with balls, which is from the Greek word for testicles — *peloné.*

Bombay   A *Bombay bowler* is a type of sun helmet or *sola topi*. The *bummalo*, a small fish found in the Indian Ocean, got its English name of *Bombay duck* from sailors' humorous perversion of the native word.

Borstal   A *Borstal* is a penal institution especially for young offenders. The *Borstal* system began in 1902, when a modified form of prison treatment for young offenders was introduced at a prison at the village of *Borstal*, near Rochester in Kent. Under the Prevention of Crime Act, of 1908, *borstal* detention became a recognized part of the penal system, separated from the prison system. Under the Criminal Justice Act of 1948, the name was changed from *borstal* detention to *borstal* training. It applies to offenders of both sexes in the 16-21 age-group.

Boston   The State capital of Massachussetts has given its name to a whist-like card-game: *boston*. Two dances, the *Boston two-step* and the *Boston waltz* also originated in the city. Thre are *Boston terriers*, and there is a haircut, a *Boston slashback.*

Bourbon County   In 1789, a Baptist minister called Elijah Craig started distilling *Bourbon* whiskey (made from a blend of corn, with malt or rye sometimes added) at Georgetown

13

in *Bourbon County*. *Bourbon County*, then in *Virginia*, now in *Kentucky*, took its name from the *Bourbon* family of European monarchs, some of whose subjects had settled in Virginia. *Bourbon* biscuits (chocolate-flavoured with a chocolate-cream filling) are not named after the place.

Brandenburg The *Brandenburg coat*, popular in the last quarter of the seventeenth century, was a long loose overcoat for men. *Brandenburg* is in East Germany, some 60km west of *Berlin*.

Brazil The lofty tree *bertholletia excelsa* forms large forests in tropical South America, including parts of *Brazil*. The ripe fruit is spherical and woody and contains numerous *brazil nuts*.

Bridport A *Bridport dagger* is a hangman's noose. The slang expression came about because the small Dorset town of *Bridport* has for many generations been a centre for the manufacture of rope, twine, net and cordage of all kinds.

Bristol For long the second city in England, in size and importance, *Bristol* has given its name to many things. *Bristol board* is fine paste-board used by artists and designers. *Bristol brick* is used for cleaning cutlery. *Bristol diamond* is a kind of rock-crystal found near the city. The term *Bristol ware* has been applied to various ceramics made there over the centuries. The sweet sherry called *Bristol milk* reflects the fact that wine from *Spain* was imported there; tradition has it that it is so called because it is the first liquid given to infants born in *Bristol*. *Bristols*, a slang word for breasts, has a peculiar connection with the place, because this is cockney rhyming slang — *Bristol Cities*/titties.

Brittany Striped sweaters called *bretons* are in imitation of the traditional garb of sailors from *Brittany*; there is also a hat called a *breton*, round-crowned with an upward-turning brim.

Brno Introduced in 1937, the *Bren* light machine-gun was standard equipment for British infantry throughout World War II. Originally it was the Czechoslovak ZB-26, designed

14

and first made at *Brno*. In Britain it was first manufactured at the small-arms factory at *Enfield*, Middlesex. The first two letters of these two place names were taken to form the weapon's name, a double-half-toponym.

Broadway The regular grid of *New York* City's avenues and streets is crossed and disturbed by the oblique *Broadway*. In one section of this long thoroughfare are many theatres; this is the reason why *Broadway* has come to mean 'New York Theatre'. This has in turn given rise to the expression '*off-Broadway*' and, further, '*off-off-Broadway*'. *Broadway* has been used in this theatrical sense since the 1880s.

Bronx The *Bronx* cocktail (gin, sweet and dry vermouth, orange juice) was invented in the Waldorf-Astoria hotel in *New York* City by a barman named Johnnie Solon. First mentioned in print in 1906, the drink is thought to have been named after the *Bronx Zoo*. The sound of contempt or derision known in Britain as a raspberry is called a *Bronx cheer* in *America*. Both these are eponymous toponyms because *The Bronx*, the northernmost of *New York's* five boroughs, was named after a seventeenth century landowner named *Jonas Bronck*.

Brunswick The *Brunswick gown* or *German gown* first became popular with ladies in Britain in 1760; it was sack-backed with long sleeves. As well as being Kings of Hanover and Great Britain and Ireland, the Hanoverian dynasty were also Dukes of *Brunswick*.

Brussels *Brassica oleracea gemmifera*, with buds like very small cabbages in the axils of its leaves, are rightly called *Brussels sprouts*, as the vegetable was developed in Belgium in the fourteenth century. Although of course known to cross-channel travellers, *Brussels sprouts* were not grown in Britain until the nineteenth century. There are also *Brussels lace* and *Brussels carpets*.

Bukhara In the past, *buckram* was a rich woven cloth, suitable for church vestments, although it can hardly have meant this when Falstaff referred (in *Henry IV, Part 1*, II. iv.) to 'rogues in *buckram* suits'. Today *buckram* means linen or

15

cotton fabric stiffened with gum or paste, and used for lining belts, collars and so on, and in bookbinding. The origin is not certain, but the word is likely to have come, through the Italian word *bucherame*, from *Bukhara*, the region of Central Asia known since the Middle Ages for its silk, cotton and carpets. *Bukhara couching* is an embroidery technique for solid filling in of designs.

Buncombe   *Bunkum* is claptrap. The expression comes from the North Carolina county of *Buncombe* and originated in the United States Congress in 1820; Representative Felix Walker, from the district, rose to speak when the House was impatiently calling for a vote. Congressman Walker persisted inopportunely, declaring that the people of his district expected it and that he was bound to 'make a speech for *Buncombe*'. *Bunkum*, frequently shortened to *bunk*, has given rise to the word *debunk*, meaning 'to remove nonsense' and thus to expose false claims or pretensions.

Burton   'Gone for a *burton*' emerged during World War II in the Royal Air Force, meaning dead, and hence missing or lost. The origin of the phrase is mysterious, defeating even Eric Partridge, who served in the RAF; his judgement was that there was probably a connection with the great brewing town of *Burton-on-Trent* in *Staffordshire*, but possibly with the outfitting firm of Montague Burton.

C

Cairngorms   *Cairngorms* are yellow or wine-coloured semi-precious stones, in fact quartz coloured by iron oxide or titanic acid. They are found in the *Cairngorm Mountains*, in the Scottish highlands.

Calicut   *Calico* is plain unbleached cotton cloth and takes its name from the sea port of *Calicut*. This was, in the sixteenth century the second port, after Goa, in *India* where Europeans called and traded. An English station was established there in 1616. Today *Calicut*, in Kerala province, is called *Kozhikode*.

Camberwell   The butterfly known to scientists as *Vanessa Antiopa* is known to collectors as the *Camberwell Beauty*. Rarely seen in Britain, this large and beautiful butterfly is common in Central and Southern Europe and in North America. It was first recorded in England in 1748 at the then rural village of *Camberwell*, now absorbed in south *London*.

Cambodia   The *Garcinia* tree, found in Thailand and *Cambodia* has gum-resin from which comes a bright yellow pigment; *gamboge* has been known in Britain for 350 years. The stuff is also, in the stately phrase of *The Oxford English Dictionary*, 'a drastic purgative'.

Cambrai   *Cambric* is fine white linen, once popular for the manufacture of handkerchiefs. It came from the Flemish town of *Cambrai*. The place used to be called *Cambray* in French and *Kamerijk* in Flemish; *cambric* rolls these two words into one. The fabric called *chambray*, a kind of gingham with a linen finish, also derives from *Cambrai*.

Cambridge   The university city of *Cambridge* has generated many fewer toponyms than *Oxford*. There are *Cambridge sausages*. There is an agricultural implement called a *Cambridge roller*. *Cambridge blue* is a lighter blue than sky-blue. *Cambridge calf* describes a method of fine bookbinding. *Cambridge chimes* were first used, in 1793, at the University Church of St Mary the Great. *Cambridge coats*, for men, first became fashionable in the 1870s.

Camden Town The London district of *Camden Town* gave its name to a coterie of artists who, influenced by W. R. Sickert (1860-1942) broke away from the New English Art Club in 1911 in shared enthusiasm for the work of Gauguin and Van Gogh. The *Camden Town Group* included Lucien Pissaro (1863-1944) and Augustus John (1883-1960); they exhibited together four times before expanding, in 1914, into the *London Group*.

Campania *Campanile*, a bell-tower, and *campanology*, the art or mystery of bells and bell-ringing both derive from the Italian word *campana*, which means bell. *Campana* comes from *Campania* the region of southern *Italy* which now comprises the provinces of Arellino, Benevento, Naples, Salerno and Caserta; *Campania* was noted for its bell-founding.

Canary Islands The *canary* or *canary finch (serinus canarius)* is found in large numbers in the Azores, in Madeira and in the *Canary Islands*. The birds have been domesticated in Europe since the sixteenth century. Madeira wine was sometimes called *Canary wine*.

Cantalupo *Cantaloupes (Cucumis melo reticulatus)* are round or oval melons, orange-fleshed and known for their sweetness. They take their delightful name from *Cantalupo in Sabina*, a town about 30 miles north of *Rome*, where there was formerly a Papal villa, and where they were first grown in Europe, in the seventeenth century, after their introduction from *Armenia*.

Canterbury A *canter* is short for *Canterbury gallop* or *Canterbury pace*. This, described as 'an easy galloping pace' or hand-gallop, refers to the pace at which mounted pilgrims are supposed to have travelled when on their way to the shrine of Thomas à Becket in *Canterbury Cathedral*. The piece of furniture called a *canterbury*, a partitioned stand for papers or music, was given this name by Thomas Sheraton, who also applied it to a partitioned supper-tray. If combined with open shelves above, it is called a *Canterbury-whatnot*.

Carlton House *Carlton House tables*, dating from the 1790s, are desk-tables and are named after those supplied to the

Prince Regent's *London* house. They are D-shaped and very elegant, and have a curved superstructure of drawers and pigeon-holes beyond the writing space. *Carlton House*, built for *Lord Carlton* in 1709, had been the Prince's home from 1783. It was demolished in 1826, the site being developed as *Carlton House Terrace* and *Carlton Gardens.*

Carmel, Mount   *Carmelite* is a light woollen fabric, named after the habits worn by members of the *Carmelite order.* This was founded in 1156 by a Calabrian named Berthold, in the *Mount Carmel* range, near Haifa, in Israel. *Carmelites,* known as White Friars, first established themselves in England in 1241.

Carrick   The *Carrick coat,* a long triple-caped dust-coat for women came into fashion about 1877. The *Carrick* district lies to the south of Ayr, in what is today the region of Strathclyde.

Carron   *Carronades* were naval guns, much used in the Napoleonic Wars, and so called because they were manufactured at the *Carron Iron Works,* near Falkirk in Scotland, from 1779. *Carron oil,* made from equal parts of linseed oil and lime water, gets its name because it was much used in the same place for treating burns.

Catacumbas   The Latin word *catacumbas* was used, from the fifth century, for the underground cemetery of the Basilica of St Sebastian, just south of *Rome.* This is the supposed burial place of both St Peter and St Paul. The meaning has extended to any similar burial place, or indeed any underground collection of cellars or galleries, as *catacombs.*

Caudebec   Originating at *Caudebec,* in Normandy, the *Caudebec hat* was a man's felt hat, imitating the beaver hat. Popular in Britain in the early eighteenth century, it was known as the *Cawdebink* or *Cordyback hat.*

Cayenne   *Cayenne pepper*, sometimes called *Guinea pepper* in the eighteenth century, comes from French Guiana, where *Cayenne,* founded in 1634, is the chief town. The powerful pepper comes from trees grown in the district. In the Tupi

language of *Brazil, cayenne* means *capsicum*, the pepper tree
Strangely enough, *cayenne pepper* is unknown in *France*.

Cerasus English took the word *cherry* from the Ol
Norman French *cherise*, mistakenly supposing that thi
word was a plural. The French word derived from the Lati
cerasum, which means 'of *Cerasus*', a place in the Roma
province of Pontus. The fruit was traditionally brought t
Rome about 100 BC by the great gourmet Lucullus. Th
province of Pontus included the Black Sea coast of moder
Turkey; Cerasus was on this coast.

Charleston The 1920s are epitomized by the *Charlestor*
the dance which emerged in that decade, and which is charac
terized by side-kicks from the knees. It took its name from
the city of *Charleston* in South Carolina, founded by th
English about 1670 and named, of course, after the reignin
English monarch, Charles II. Fort Sumter, the capture c
which in April 1861 may be said to have started the America
Civil War, is at *Charleston*.

Charolais The large white cattle called *Charolais* take the
name from a region of eastern *France*; once an isolate
Habsburg possession, *Charolais* is in the Burgundy distric
In recent years *Charolais* cattle have become popular all ove
the world with cattle-breeders because they grow fast an
are heavily muscled.

Chartreuse The green-yellow liqueur is herb-flavoure
brandy and was invented and made by the monks of *La Grand*
Chartreuse. This is the head monastery of the *Carthusia*
order, some 12 miles north of Grenoble in the French *Alps*
First made in the seventeenth century, *chartreuse* was no
sold commercially until 200 years later. It was a strange in
vention for such a strict and austere order as the *Carthusian*
Charterhouse is the anglicized form of *Chartreuse*.

Cheshire Although the phrase 'to grin like a *Cheshire* ca
has been in use for at least 200 years, the origin is unknow
The county gave its name to *Cheshire cheese*, which has bee
popular since the sixteenth century. There is also a roug
country dance called a *Cheshire round*.
20

Cheviot *Cheviot sheep*, a short-woolled hardy breed, take their name from the *Cheviot Hills*, on the English–Scottish border. *Cheviot cloth*, a woollen or *worsted* fabric, takes its name from the wool.

Chevy Chase To *chivvy* is to badger or to harass. The word dates from the seventeenth century and derives from *Chevy Chase*. *The Ballad of Chevy Chase* is a well known ballad dating from the fifteenth century. The poem celebrates a famous skirmish in the Border country, the scene of many affrays in years of Anglo-Scottish cross-border raids in which the Percy and Douglas families were prominent on the English and Scottish sides respectively. *Chevy* is another name for the game 'prisoner's base'.

Chicago The naval multiple pom-pom, a rapid-firing anti-aircraft gun much used in World War II was known as a *Chicago piano*. The nickname arose because machine guns had been used in gang-land battles in the 1920s in *Chicago*. Similarly a *Chicago sundae*, made with ice-cream and pineapple, got its name because hand-grenades were also sometimes used in those days, and were known locally as 'pineapples'. On the other hand the *Chicago* style of jazz, which also developed in the city in the 1920s, has no connection with organized crime; the style is typified by the playing of Eddie Condon.

China *China* is probably the most widespread and most frequently used toponym. The familiar earthenware of a fine semi-transparent texture was first brought to Europe in the sixteenth century by the Portuguese, who called it porcelain. In Britain it soon became known as *china-ware* or *cheney-ware*. Manufacture started in England in the eighteenth century. *Crêpe de chine*, the silky crêpe which evokes *Chinese* delicacy, has no real connection with *China*. The phrase 'all Lombard Street to a *china* orange', indicating extraordinarily long odds, is strange. *China*, or sweet, oranges were a great delicacy from the sixteenth century onwards, when they began to replace earlier Middle Eastern oranges, which were sour. Pepys notes the arrival of a box of *china oranges* on 16 February 1660, for his patron and kinsman,

21

the first Earl of Sandwich; they must have become very cheap for the phrase to make sense. To refer to a friend as a *china*, however, is cockney rhyming-slang: *china plate*/mate.

Christiania A *christi*, or *christiania turn*, is a highly skilled mid-air turn, swing or change of direction, practised by expert skiers. The expression, current since the turn of the century, comes from *Christiania*, the name of the Norwegian capital before it was changed to Oslo in 1925. *Norway* of course, was the home of skiing long before it became popular in *Switzerland* and thence around the world.

Citeaux The *Cistercian order* takes its name from the place where it was founded in 1098. This is *Citeaux* (*Cistercium* in Latin) near *Dijon*, eastern *France*. The *Cistercians* would today be called a break-away movement from the Benedictines. The austerities they practised were so extreme that the order did not flourish until the arrival of the inspiring St Bernard in 1112. The first English house was founded at Waverley, Surrey in 1128.

Cleveland The *Cleveland Bay* breed of working horses is the oldest-established in England, taking its name from the area, now a county, in north-eastern England; the *Cleveland* horse is always a bay — that is, reddish-brown in colour.

Clink *Clink*, meaning prison, comes from a famous *London* prison, in *Clink Street*, Southwark, which was destroyed in the Gordon Riots of 1780. It is possible that the street picked up its name from the prison, as the word might be descriptive of the sound made in a prison when chains were much used. It would be pleasant to record that there was a magistrate's court in Beak Street, Soho, giving rise to the use of 'beak' for magistrate; but, alas, the nearest magistrate's court was, and remains, in Bow Street.

Cluny The *Cluniac* order of monks and nuns derive their name from the place where their order was established in 910. This was *Cluny*, in Burgundy. The first *Cluniac* house in England was founded in 1077, at Lewes, Sussex.

Clydesdale Originally bred in the valley of the *Clyde*, the heavy and powerful draught horses known as *Clydesdales*
22

have been noted for their strength and endurance; *Clydesdales* were the prime agricultural working horses of *Scotland.*

Coalport *Coalport* porcelain takes its name from the Shropshire town, where a factory was founded by John Rose in 1796; it moved to *Staffordshire* in 1926. The factory produced both decorative and domestic porcelain, famous for its highly translucent glaze.

Coburg The *coburg loaf* (of bread) was introduced in Britain shortly after Queen Victoria had, in 1840, married Prince Albert of Saxe-*Coburg*-Gotha. Similarly, a material called *coburg* was promoted, as we would now say, at the same time: this was a thin fabric of worsted and cotton or worsted and silk, twilled on one side. The *coburg carriage*, a two-wheeled covered affair, was an earlier invention.

Concord The *Concord coach*, an American vehicle, took its name from *Concord*, New Hampshire where it was developed. *Concord coaches* were used as stage and mail coaches all over *America.*

Conestoga A *stogie* is a long, rough cigar, in *America.* The word comes from the town of *Conestoga*, in Lancaster County, Pennsylvania. The same town also gave its name to the *Conestoga wagon.* This was a famous vehicle, first made in the mid-eighteenth century and much used in the westward migrations of the next century, when it was generally known as a covered wagon or prairie schooner.

Congo The *conga* (a file of people, repeating three steps and a kick) is a Latin-American dance which underlines the influence of Africa on the Americas, as the name is taken from the *Congo*, the great river which flows into the South Atlantic. The *congo hair-style*, popular in both Africa and the Caribbean, is well explained by its alternative name of *corn-row.*

Connemara Ponies of the *Connemara* breed are said to have some Spanish blood mixed with their native Irish; they are large, and often used as polo ponies.

23

Cordova *Cordovan* was high-class flexible goatskin shoe-leather from *Cordoba*, the *Spanish* city anglicised as *Cordova*. The same word was also used to refer to dressed vegetable-tanned leather made from the part of a horse-hide known as the shell, used for razor-strops. *Cordovan* was also known as *crup* and as *cordwain*. A *cordwainer* is a shoemaker. The Worshipful Company of *Cordwainers* stands twenty-seventh in precedence in the Livery Companies of the City of *London*.

Corinth The Old English name for *currants* was *raisins of Corauntz*, from the French *raisins de Coraunte*, that is 'of *Corinth*'. From describing raisins made from seedless grapes, the word went on to be used for the small round berries of certain species of *ribes*, such as *black-currants* and *red-currants*.

Corsica The *Corsican pine (Pinus nigra maritima)* a fast-growing species, was introduced to Britain, from *Corsica*, in 1759.

Cos The long-leaved *cos lettuce (lactuca sativa longifolia)* is so called because it was introduced into Britain, in the seventeenth century, from the Greek island of *Cos* or *Kos*, which lies close to the Turkish coast opposite Budrum. John Evelyn (1620-1706), a keen gardener, mentions the variety in his diary for 1699.

Coventry To send to *Coventry* is to ignore somebody, to make him or her feel disgraced. The phrase is said to have originated from the great dislike in which soldiers were held by the citizens of *Coventry*; this was so intense that any woman seen speaking to a soldier was at once ostracized by the rest of the population. The word *coventrate* did not survive World War II. It was taken from the German *coventrieren*, meaning to attack and devastate an area by aerial bombardment, and aptly describes what was done by the Luftwaffe at *Coventry* on the night of 14/15 November 1940.

Cremona A *cremona* is a violin of the highest class, made at this town in *Lombardy*, where the art of making superb violins reached its highest perfection in the seventeenth and
24

and early eighteenth centuries; it is where the Stradivari, Amati and Guarneri families of violin-makers lived and worked. Sometimes organs have *cremona* stops; this, however, has nothing to do with the violins or the place, as this is a corruption of the German *krummhorn*, crooked horn. In this sense, therefore, *cremona* is a spurious toponym.

Crete   The word *quince* has a long and complex history. The tree, a native of Asia, was first recorded in *Crete*, known in ancient times as *Cydonia*. *Quinces* were introduced into Roman *Italy*, where they were called *malum cydonium* (Cretan apples). *Malum* dropped away, and a Latin variant, *cotoneum*, became the Old French *cooin.* This became *coyn* or *quine* in Middle English. Finally *quine* became *quince*. In embroidery, there is a *Cretan* stitch.

Creton   *Cretonne* is stout unglazed cotton cloth printed in colours or patterns on one or both sides. It takes its name from the Normandy village of *Creton*.

Croatia   *Croatia*, today a region of northern Yugoslavia, was a place which provided many mercenary soldiers in the seventeenth century. *Croatian* soldiers wore scarves. These were taken up as a fashion in *France*, where they were called *cravate* (French for *Croatian*). The fashion travelled to Britain in due course, the word being anglicized as *cravat*.

Culross   Known elsewhere as griddles, the thin iron plates on which oatcakes, scones etc are cooked, are known in *Scotland* as girdles. *Culross girdles* are, or were, the best. *Culross* is in Fife Region.

Cyprus   The origins of the word *copper* lie in the Latin *cyprium* and the Greek *kuprios*; both these words mean 'of *Cyprus*'. In the ancient world, *Cyprus* was the chief source of *copper*. The cypress tree is by way of being a spurious toponym: it has nothing to do with the island etymologically.

D

Dalmatia   A *dalmatic* is an ecclesiastical, sometimes a royal, vestment; it has a split on both sides of the skirt and wide sleeves and is marked with two stripes. It is so named because it evolved in *Dalmatia*, now part of the coastal region of Yugoslavia, which also gave its name to *Dalmatian dogs*.

Damascus   *Damask*, a rich silk fabric with elaborate designs originally came from the city of *Damascus*. The embroidery technique known as *Damask-darning* first evolved as a method of darning *damask* materials. *Damson* is short for *Damascene plum*, the small plums which were first grown in and around *Damascus*.

Dartmoor   The hardy and lovable *Dartmoor* breed of pony is well known; as is the equally hardy *Dartmoor* breed of sheep.

Delft   *Delft* is the glazed earthenware which has been made at *Delft*, in *Holland* since the fourteenth century.

Denmark   A *Danish* or a *Danish pastry* is a rolled pastry filled with cheese, prunes, or nuts etc. Although no doubt originating in *Denmark*, a *Danish* today has strong *New York* associations. The *Danish Landrace* breed of pigs, crossed with the *Large White Yorkshire*, may be said today to dominate European pig-rearing. *Danish trousers*, with legs that ended just below the knees, became popular wear for boys in the 1870s. In the late eighteenth century, tricorne hats turned up at the back and down in front were called *Danish cocks*.

Denver   The *Denver boot* or *clamp*, introduced by the *London* Metropolitan Police in 1983 to penalize parking offenders, is so called because it was pioneered by the authorities of *Denver*, Ohio. The clamp, fixed to a wheel of a vehicle, immobilizes it and can only be removed with much trouble and some expense.

Demerara   The yellowish-brown crystallized demerara sugar comes from the Demerara district of Guyana. The district takes its name from the *Demerara River*, which flows into the Atlantic at the capital, Georgetown.

Deolali *Doolally*, a countryman's word for feeble-mindedness is an import from *India*. On arrival in *India*, troops were often first sent to a transit camp at *Deolali*, about 100 miles north-east of *Bombay*. Military mental patients were also assembled there, on their way home to the Netley Mental Hospital. *Deolali-tap* accordingly came to mean, in the Army in *India*, 'a bit round the bend' and the expression found its way back to England in the nineteenth century.

Derby About 1750 a factory was established at *Derby* for the manufacture of soft-paste porcelain; its products are known as *Derby porcelain*. From 1786 to 1811 the fine porcelain called *Crown Derby* (because of its mark) was produced. This factory closed in 1848. *The Royal Crown Derby Porcelain Company* was established in *Derby* in 1876. Both *Derby* hats and the Epsom *Derby* take their name from Earls of *Derby*, not from the place.

Derbyshire A *Derbyshire desk* is a simple writing box rather than a desk. Often of oak, with carved sides, they were in general use in the seventeenth century and earlier, for transporting papers and books. *Derbyshire neck* is a kind of goitre. The *Derbyshire gritstone* breed of sheep is named after the rocky outcrops in the county.

Devon As well as the *Dartmoor* breed, the *South Devon* and the *Devon longwool* breeds of sheep are natives of *Devon*.

Dijon Roses are often, indeed usually, named after individual people. The fine climbing rose *Gloire de Dijon*, however, takes its name from the town of *Dijon*, in the French *département* of Côte-d'Or.

Dishley *Dishley Leicester* sheep take their name from the village of *Dishley*, where Robert Bakewell (1725-95) began breeding them in about 1750.

Donegal *Donegal tweed* comes from *County Donegal*, the most northerly county of Eire, to the north-west of *Ulster*.

27

Dongari Killa   Today *dungarees* are overalls of the trousers-bib-and-braces type. Originally the word meant a cheap and inferior type of cotton cloth from which such garments were made. The Hindi word *dungri*, comes from *Dongari Kapar* a term used for the country cloth sold in the quarter around *Dongari Killa*, the local name for Fort George, Bombay.

Downing Street   Because the Foreign & Commonwealth Office and the official residences of the Prime Minister and of the Chancellor of the Exchequer are in *Downing Street*, it can be regarded as the centre of the British Government, and is treated as such by the media (*'Downing Street* says ... '). It takes its name from Sir George Downing (?1623-1684) Member of Parliament, Exchequer official, ambassador and entrepreneur, who undertook a building development in the street in 1682. Downing had the distinction of being the second man to graduate from Harvard University. His grandson founded Downing College, Cambridge.

Dresden   *Dresden china* was the term applied in eighteenth century Britain to *Meissen* porcelain; *Meissen* is some 15 miles from *Dresden*, in *Saxony*, East Germany.

Duffel   *Duffle* or *duffel* is coarse woollen cloth, named after the place where it was first manufactured, the town of *Duffel*, on the Nethe river, near Antwerp in Belgium. It is most familiar in the USA in the form of *duffle-bags*, cylindrical bags for personal belongings, now made of canvas. In Britain it is more familiar in *duffle-coats*, short coats with hoods, fastened with toggles, once official issue in the Royal Navy.

Dumdum   *Dumdum* (expanding) bullets were so called because they were first made at the military cantonment of *Dumdum*, Calcutta.

Duren   Invented in 1906, *duralumin* was for many years the strongest of aluminium alloys. It was first produced, and named by, the *Durener* Metallwerke Aktien Gesellschaft. The manufacturing town of *Duren* lies between Aachen and Cologne.

Durham The *Durham* or Shorthorn breed of cattle, developed by the Colling brothers in *Scotland* in the early years of the nineteenth century was the first to have an organized Breed Society, with whom all members of the breed were registered. It was from this breed that the Dairy Shorthorn was developed.

E

Eaton Hall   *Eaton Hall chairs*, round easy-chairs in use from the 1850s, got their name when chairs of this pattern were supplied to the first Duke of Westminster at *Eaton Hall, Cheshire* in 1867.

Eccles   Containing the same ingredients as *Banbury* cake, but usually round, *Eccles cake* was made and popularized at the Lancashire town which is today in part a suburb of Manchester.

Egham, Staines and Windsor   A cumbersome early nineteenth century nickname for the tricorne hat was *Egham, Staines and Windsor*, from the triangular geographical situation of these three towns.

Egypt   The race of wanderers known in Britain as *gipsies* are of Indian origin. They first reached England in the sixteenth century; they were popularly supposed to have come from *Egypt*, and were named accordingly. Other European countries made the same assumption: *gipsies* are *gitano* in *Spain,* *gyptenaer* in *Holland* — but comparison with *Bohemia* is instructive. The word *gipsy* (or *gypsy*) gave rise to the verb to *gip*, to cheat.

El-Fustat   *Fustian* has meant different things over the centuries. Once it meant a coarse cloth made of cotton and flax; then a thick twilled cotton cloth with a short nap and usually died a dark colour; *fustian* today is variously known as velveteen, corduroy or moleskin. The original material was made in the Cairo district of *El-Fustat.*

Elvas   *Elvas* is a fortified frontier city in central Portugal. It is noted for its plums which, preserved and crystallized, were once famous throughout Europe, and were much consumed at Christmas time.

Enfield   The *sten gun* was a sub-machine gun or machine pistol used by British and Allied forces in World War II. It is half a toponym, as the word is formed from the initials of the surnames of its inventors (Sheppard and Turpin) and
30

the first syllable of the place of its original manufacture, *Enfield.*

England   The *English elm (Ulmus procera)* deserves its name — it is to be found only in Britain. Since the advent of 'Dutch' elm disease, its numbers have been greatly reduced.

Epsom   A mineral spring at *Epsom* (a corruption of *Ebbisham*) was discovered in 1618 and caused the place to become the most considerable spa in seventeenth century *England*, primarily for the citizens of *London*. From 1675, magnesium sulphate was made there by evaporation from the spring water, and thus became known as *Epsom salt(s)*; the words went on to be used generally for magnesium suphate, however made.

Essex   The *Essex Saddleback* breed of pigs is a hardy one, and is noted for its pork and bacon.

Eton   *Eton collars* were stiff white collars of great depth, worn overlapping the jacket; *Eton jackets*, nicknamed 'bum-freezers', were shortened jackets. Both were worn by the smallest boys at *Eton College. Eton crops,* a female hair-style which apparently imitated male hair, first became modish in the 1920s.

Euston Road   Sir William Coldstream (b.1908) started a School of Drawing and Painting in *London's Euston Road* in the 1930s. Its activities came to an end with the out-break of World War II. The name, however, was given to a group of post-Impressionist realistic painters, including Coldstream, Victor Pasmore, Claude Rogers and Graham Bell.

Exmoor   Both the *Exmoor* breed of pony and the *Exmoor Horn* breed of sheep take their names from the North Devon upland.

31

F

Faenza   In Europe generally *faience* is the name given to tin-glazed earthenware made in *France, Germany, Spain* and Scandinavia; in Britain *faience* equates with *delftware*. In both senses the word comes from the French word *faience*, 'of *Faenza*'. *Faenza*, near Ravenna, has been prominent in the Italian ceramic industry since the sixteenth century.

Fair Isle   Woollen garments knitted with certain designs characteristic of *Fair Isle* have been popular throughout Britain for about 150 years. *Fair Isle* is one of the *Shetland* Islands.

Fez   Shaped like an inverted flower-pot, and usually a shade of red, the tasselled, brimless hats were worn in Muslim countries especially *Turkey* (until banned there by the modernizing Kemal Atatürk). The *fez* takes its name from the sacred Islamic city of *Fez*, or *Fès*, in Morocco, where they were once made. Full Muhammadan devotions involve placing the forehead on the ground, something that cannot be done in a hat with a brim, but is feasible in a turban or a *fez*.

Findhorn/Findon   *Finnan Haddock*, smoked haddock, is traditionally said to come from one of two seaport villages in *Scotland: Findon* near *Aberdeen*, or *Findhorn*, on the Moray Firth. The former place has closer connections with sea-fishing.

Flanders   *Flemish bond* is a brick-laying technique, a style of overlapping; *flemish eyes* are nautical knots; *flemish coils* are ropes coiled in a particular way (giving rise to the verb 'to *flemish*'. All take their appellations from *Flanders*.

Florence   Gold coins, decorated with lilies, were first struck in *Florence* in 1252; they soon found their way around Europe, where they were sometimes called *florences*, and to Britain, where they were known as *florins*. A hundred years later the same word was used for gold coins worth one third of a pound, struck under Edward III (1327-1377). The word was used again in 1849, when the first two-shilling pieces were

32

minted, as the first step towards decimalization of the pound, something not put into effect until 15 February 1971. *Florin* refers not only to *Florence*, but perhaps also to the coin's original local nickname: *fiorino*, little flower. In the nineteenth century, cloth-covered buttons were sometimes called *Florentine buttons*. There is a *Florentine* embroidery stitch. There are *florentine* biscuits, *florentine* material, *florence* (pie), *florence* flasks and *Florence* fennel.

France   Both male and female fashions started coming from *France* many years ago. *French hoods*, for women, and *French sleeves*, for men, date from the sixteenth century, while *French cloaks, cuffs* and *pockets*, all for men, date from the seventeenth century. There are also *French heels, French knots, French pleats* and *French seams. French windows, French polish, French chalk* and *French horns* also all came from *France. French leave* (unpermitted absence) and *French letters* (condoms) are not accurately assigned to *France*; nor is *French cricket*. Red-legged partridges are called *Frenchmen*, because the *French* Army of the late nineteenth century wore blue tunics and red trousers.

Friesland   The familiar black-and-white *Friesian* cattle were originally bred in the *Friesland* province in northern *Holland*.

G

Gaza *Gauze*, very thin transparent fabric which can be made of silk, linen or cotton, is a word derived from the French *gaze*; this is thought to come from *Gaza*, in Israel the place of its origin.

Geneva *Geneva bands*, twin white strips dependent from the collar, worn by clergymen, lawyers and others were introduced to Britain by the seventeenth century Puritans emulating those worn by the Calvinists of *Geneva*. *Gin* is short for *Geneva*, the original English name for the spirit Confusion arose because *gin* is flavoured with juniper berries and the French for juniper is *genevre*.

Genoa *Genoa jibs*, or *genoas*, have been popular sails in racing yachts since the 1930s. They take their name from the Italian port, as do *Genoa treacle, Genoa velvet, Genoa lettuce, Genoa cake* (rich currant cake with almonds on top), and *paste of Genoa* (a baked sweetmeat made from quince, spices and sugar). Twilled cotton cloth, made in *Genoa*, was known in the sixteenth century in Britain as *jenes fustian*; this was later shortened to *jeanes* and to *jeans*.

Germany Known to doctors as *rubella, German measles,* a mild form of measles, is so named because '*German*' was at one time used to mean 'spurious'. *German silver*, for example, was in fact an alloy of nickel, zinc and copper.

Geysir *Maughan's Patent Geyser*, was the first piece of apparatus of its kind. Dating from the 1870s, it was a gas-operated appliance for the rapid heating of water for baths and other domestic purposes. Many other types of *geyser* followed. The name came from the word *geyser*, meaning a hot spring, which in turn comes from *Geysir*, a famous hot spring in *Iceland* which intermittently throws up a column of hot water.

Ghetto This word, one of the saddest in any language, now describes any compulsory enclave for an ethnic group.

34

Originally the only *ghettos* were those established in many European cities for Jews. The first of all these places was in *Venice*. The first Jews in that city lived on Giudecca, which may have been named after them. In the sixteenth century Jews were confined in a walled and guarded part of the city. The word may come from the medieval Venetian for iron-founding, as there had been a foundry on the site of this first *ghetto*; it may be derived from *borghetto* (little town); or it may come from *Aegyptus*, Latin for *Egypt*.

Glasshouse (S) The Army's Detention Barracks in Aldershot Command, at Woking, had a partly glassed roof. Its nickname *The Glasshouse*, came to be applied to any military prison or detention centre.

Glastonbury *Glastonbury chairs* are folding wooden chairs, first made in the sixteenth century in imitation of the Abbot of *Glastonbury*'s chair preserved at Wells. *Glastonbury thorn Crataegus oxyacantha)* is an early flowering variety of hawthorn, supposedly in flower at Christmas. There is a legend that it sprang from the staff of Joseph of Arimathea, who is believed to have come to *Glastonbury* about AD 61 and to have built the first church there. *Glastonbury muffs* were designed to keep the feet warm in coaches and open motor-cars, and were first made in *Glastonbury*.

Glen Garry The Highland cap known as the *glengarry*, higher at the front than at the back, was adopted by several Scottish regiments. *Glen Garry* is in Highland Region.

Gloucestershire The *Gloucestershire Old Spot* breed of pigs is an old one, but the records only go back to 1913.

Goldsmiths' Hall *Hallmarks* are properly the official sets of marks or stamps used at *Goldsmiths' Hall*, in London, by The Goldsmiths' Company to mark the standard of the gold and silver articles assayed there. The practice dates from the year 1300, when a statute of Edward I decreed that all silver wares were to be tested by the Goldsmiths' Guild and marked accordingly. *Hallmark* is used also to describe similar marks used in Government Assay offices. The word has gone on to be applied to any mark or standard of genuineness, excellence or worth.

Greece *Verdigris* can be made artificially, but occur naturally as rust on *copper*; it is much used as a pigment. Th name comes from the Old French *vert de Grèce ('green c Greece')*. As *copper* derives from *Cyprus*, where it was onc mostly found, it might have been more logical to have calle the stuff *'verdicyp'* . . .

Grub Street According to Samuel Johnson, *Grub Stree* was 'originally the name of a street near Moorfields in *Londor* much inhabited by writers of small histories, dictionaries, an temporary poems, whence any mean production is calle *grub street'*. In the nineteenth century, the name was altere to Milton Street, Cripplegate; but the old name survives a an epithet implying literary hack-work.

Guernsey A *guernsey* is a type of thick knitted sweate: originally for seamen. There are also *Guernsey cattle*. Bot *Guernsey* and *Jersey* in the Channel Islands have the di tinction of having both cattle and sweaters named after then

Guinea *Guineas* were once the chief English gold coin: They were struck from 1663 to 1813 and had a value c twenty shillings until 1717, when it was altered to twenty one. *Guineas* had been struck 'in the name of and for the us of The Company of Royal Adventurers trading with Africa at the time called the *Guinea* trade, this being the curren name for West Africa. Sovereigns replaced *guineas* from 181? but *guineas* remained fashionable long after the coins ha vanished, for professional fees, and for bloodstock and othe auctions. *Guinea-fowl* originated in West Africa; but *guinea pigs* did not — they came from South America, but wer carried in *Guineamen*, ships trading normally with Wes Africa. There is a *Guinea* hair style, popular in Africa an the West Indies.

H

ackney (S) *Hackney* is not, as might be supposed, a toponym ‌derived from the *London* borough of *Hackney*. The word ‌first meant a riding-horse (as opposed to a hunter or a ‌draught-horse) and came from the Old French *haquenée*, ‌which meant an ambling horse, especially for women to ride. *Hackney* went on to mean a hired-out horse. This was often ‌shortened to *hack* from which came the verb to *hack*, to ride. ‌Further meanings developed, including *hackney-carriage*, a ‌hired carriage, the official name for *London* taxicabs to this ‌day; and hack-work, donkey-work done by somebody hired ‌for the purpose; and hack, a literary drudge.

Harris *Harris tweed*, renowned world-wide for its long-‌lasting qualities and its strength, comes from the island of *Harris*, in the Outer Hebrides.

Havana Many smokers consider *Havana* cigars to be the ‌finest in the world. The soil, temperature and humidity of ‌Cuba combine to create ideal tobacco-growing conditions; ‌the completed cigars are exported from the Cuban capital, *Habana*, known in English as *Havana* or, in times past, *Havannah*.

Helos A *helot* is a serf or slave. Originally *helots* were a ‌particular class of serf in ancient *Sparta*, after the inhabitants ‌of the *Laconian* town of *Helos* had been forced into slavery.

Henley The *Henley boater* was briefly popular in the 1890s, ‌taking its name from the *Henley* Regatta. It was the same ‌shape of hat as a straw boater, but made of blue or drab felt.

Herefordshire *Herefords*, the red-coated, white-marked cattle ‌first bred in *Herefordshire*, are to be found today in cattle-‌raising districts around the world.

Hesse *Hessian* is coarse, strong cloth made from hemp and ‌jute, originally coming from the Grand Duchy of *Hesse*. In *America* especially, *hessian* means a mercenary soldier; this ‌is because, in the War of Independence, the British employed ‌some 30,000 *Hessian* mercenaries. *Hessian boots*, once much

37

used by soldiers, became fashionable footwear in the early nineteenth century.

Highlands The *Highlands* of *Scotland* have given their name to *Highland cattle*, shaggy and long-horned. *Highland ponies* are a breed unequalled for hardiness and staying-power. The *Highland fling*, a very spirited dance, also comes from the area.

Hocheim Today *hock* is loosely applied to many German white wines. It is, in fact, a shortened version of *hockamore*, a rather feeble Anglicization of *hocheimer*, the wine of *Hocheim*, a place on the Main, in the Rheingau district of *Hesse*-Nassau.

Holland Rye-based *gin* from *Holland* is called *Hollands*, retaining the *s*, because it represents *hollandsch genever*. There is also a linen fabric called *holland*: when unbleached it was called *brown holland*, and was much used for dust-covers in Victorian days. *In dutch* means, especially in *America*, 'in disgrace'; *Dutch courage* (achieved by the use of alcohol); *double dutch* (incomprehensible language); *Dutch comfort* (highly uncomfortable) and *Dutch uncle* (self-appointed adviser) are all pejorative expressions dating from Anglo-Dutch trade rivalry and wars of the seventeenth century, but it has to be recalled the *Dutch* and *Deutsch* (German) were often confused in those days. *Dutch auctions, Dutch treat* (shared expenses), *Dutch barns* (sideless) and *Dutch caps* (pessaries) are other ways in which the Netherlands have invaded the English language. There is also a blight which kills elm trees called *'Dutch elm disease'*. 'My old Dutch' however has nothing to do with *Holland*: it is Cockney rhyming slang: Duchess of Fife/wife.

Homburg King Edward VII, when Prince of Wales, was a leader of fashion. Each year he took a 'cure' at a continental *spa*; his favourite resort was *Bad Homburg*, just to the north of *Frankfurt*. When there he would wear an 'informal' type of hat, which thus got the name of *Homburg*. This occurred in the late 1880s. It was repopularized in the 1930s by Anthony Eden, then a young and dapper Cabinet Minister, later first Earl of Avon; the *homburg* is sometimes called an 'Anthony Eden'.

38

Hong Kong The garment known as a *Hong Kong sheath*, or 'cheongsam', is straight, high-collared, short-sleeved, of silk or cotton and has a slit on one side of the skirt. Fine seams are sometimes given a *haute-couture Hong Kong* finish.

Honiton Until it was by-passed, *Honiton*, some 16 miles north-east of Exeter, was for many years notorious for its enormous summer-holiday traffic-jams. It was equally famed for *Honiton lace*, from the days, in Elizabeth I's reign, when Flemish immigrants first settled there to ply their trade as lace-makers.

Hungary *Pomade hongroise* was a preparation for twirling the ends of a moustache into fine, permanent, horizontal spikes. *Hungarian stitches* are used in canvas-work to fill in backgrounds.

I

Iceland Ponies of the *Icelandic* breed are, not surprisingly, very hardy; they have their own gait, which is faster and smoother than a trot.

India *India paper*, much used for bibles and prayer-books, is very thin, but strong and opaque. Made in imitation of paper imported from *China* it was called *India paper* as a means of promoting it. *Indian ink* likewise imitates Chinese, or Japanese, imports. *India-rubber*, on the other hand, first came from South America, getting its name from the West Indies. Bottle-shaped *Indian clubs* resemble American *Indian* weapons. *Indian file* is named after the North American *Indian* practice: walking or marching in single file was the only practicable way of traversing the forests. Only the autumn warm weather known as an *Indian summer* is named after the *Indian* sub-continent.

Inverness An *Inverness cloak* had a removable part, called an *Inverness cape*. Both were named after the town where they were chiefly manufactured, from about 1860 until World War I.

Italy *Italic*, meaning 'of *Italy*', is the name given to the sloped printing characters used for words in foreign languages, names of ships, for emphasis, and for other purposes. They were the invention of the famous Italian printer Aldus Manutius (?1450-1515). Originally an economy measure, they were first used in his small edition of Virgil, published in 1501. *Italics* were designed to imitate hand-writing, probably 'Chancery hand' — the elegant writing used in the Papal Chancery. *Italics* were introduced to Britain in 1528 by Wynkyn de Worde (d. 1534), the apprentice of and successor to William Caxton (?1422-1491). In the late eighteenth century women's shoes sometimes had *Italian heels*, small peg-tops set forward of the back of the shoe.

J

Japan   Charles II and his court had developed a taste for flamboyant furnishings during their exile (1651-1660). Imported *Chinese* lacquer was much in demand in Restoration *England*, but the supply was limited. *Chinese* and *Japanese* lacquer depended on the gum of a small *Chinese* tree, *rhus vernicifera*. This was lacking in Europe, but cabinet-makers succeeded in producing imitation lacquers such as shellac. The first manual for copying Far Eastern lacquer was published in 1688; the process was known as *japanning*. The *Japanese larch (latrix kaempferi)* was introduced to Britain, from the mountains of *Japan*, in 1861.

Jerez de la Frontera   Fortified wine imported into Britain from the early sixteenth century from the Spanish port of *Jerez de la Frontera* was called *sherris-sack*. '*Sherris*' was an attempt to render *Jerez* into English. In Shakespeare's day, the drink was known as *sack*; it was about his consumption of *sack* that Falstaff was teased by the future king in *Henry IV*. *Sack* was probably a mis-hearing of the French word *sec* (dry). The word *sherry* evolved later, it being mistakenly supposed that *sherris* was a plural word.

Jerico   *Jerry-built*, a Victorian expression, means unsubstantially built, or built from poor materials. It derives from *Jericho*, where the city walls collapsed when shouted at; the episode is described in Joshua 6: 1-21.

Jersey   The Channel Island of *Jersey* has given its name to *Jersey cattle*. It has also provided the name for the sweaters called *jerseys*, as well as to the knitted *jersey* material, first used for making *jerseys*. The State of *New Jersey* in the USA is the origin of *Jersey justice*, which was popularly supposed to be both swift and severe. *Jersey wagons*, low-slung basket-carriages, were first made there. Presumably the same applies to *Jersey lightning* — applejack.

Jerusalem (S)   The *Jerusalem* artichoke has nothing to do with the Holy Land, and is not an artichoke. It is the tuber of a native American sunflower (*helianthus tuberosus*) and was introduced to Europe in the garden in *Rome* of Cardinal

Farnese about 1617. It reached *England* three years later; the Italian word for sunflower — *girasole* — was lazily anglicized as *Jerusalem*.

Jodhpur *Jodpurs* are simplified riding-gear; by including close-fitting legs with breeches, the need for high boots or gaiters is dispensed with (although there are *jodhpur boots*). Plainly the name comes from the town and district of *Jodhpur* in Rajasthan, north-west *India*; it has been in use since the turn of the century. It is, perhaps, possible that the word is eponymous rather than toponymous, as the garments may have been popularized by a Maharajah of *Jodhpur*.

Jura The geological term *Jurassic*, indicating 'the presence, in considerable quantities, of granular limestone' derives from the *Jura* mountains, on the Franco-Swiss border.

K

Kansas City   The *Kansas City* style of jazz is best exemplified by the playing of Bill ('Count') Basie (1904-1983).

Kaoling, Mount   *Kaolin* is a fine white clay produced by the decomposition of feldspar and used in the manufacture of porcelain. It can be dug in many places, but originally came from *China*, and takes its name from the *Kaoling* mountain in northern *China*, where it was first obtained.

Kasaba   *Casaba* is a variety of winter melon with yellow skin and sweet white flesh. The name comes from the Turkish town of *Kasaba*, now Turgutlu.

Kentucky   The state of *Kentucky* has given its name to the world-famous, romantic-sounding but hard-wearing *Kentucky blue grass*. At the time of the War of Independence, the *Kentucky hunting rifle* was the finest small-arms weapon in the world.

Kersey   *Kersey* is twilled woollen cloth; it has a smooth face, soft nap and diagonally ribbed appearance. It originated in the *Suffolk* village of *Kersey*.

Kimberley   Named in 1866, *kimberlite* is the eruptive rock, or 'blue ground' which is the matrix of the diamonds of *Kimberley*, South Africa and elsewhere. Diamonds were first discovered at *Kimberley* in 1870; the town got its name from the British statesman, the first Earl of Kimberley (1826-1902).

Kimblewick   Horses are controlled primarily by the bit in their mouths. Snaffles are jointed bits; a *Kimblewick snaffle* is named after the hamlet in the Vale of Aylesbury where the deviser had his stables.

Kocs   There are very few instances in the English language of words from *Hungary*, but this is certainly one of them. *Coach*, and the equivalent word in all European languages, all come from the Magyar *kocsi*; this means 'of *Kocs*', a place south of Komorn, between Raab and Buda where, from the late fifteenth century, *kocsi szeker*, or *Kocs* wagons, the first-ever *coaches* were made. The first to be made in Britain was for the Earl of Rutland, in 1555, by Walter Rippon, who also made a *coach* for Queen Elizabeth I. It is tempting to suppose that the word went on to mean tutor, and later a teacher of sport, as in cricket *coach*, because young gentlemen setting off on the Grand Tour by *coach*, were often accompanied, shepherded and bear-led by a tutor.

Kremlin Many ancient Russian cities have a *kremlin*; the word, of Tartar origin, means 'citadel'. The *Kremlin* in *Moscow*, the seat of the Russian government, often has acts or opinions attributed to it.

Knole The Sackville family's seat in Kent, *Knole*, just outside Sevenoaks, has a particular type of settee, dating from about 1615. It is straight-backed with semi-adjustable sides secured with cords; it is velvet-covered and of beech-wood. Settees of this pattern were much copied by cabinet-makers and were marketed as *Knole settees*.

L

Laburinthos (F) The word *labyrinth* comes from a place-name, although the place is mythical. It comes from the Greek *laburinthos*, which was the name given to the maze-like structure in *Crete*, made by Daedalus, and occupied by the Minotaur, a fabulous monster, half bull and half man, the offspring of Pasiphae, wife of Minos, king of *Crete*, and a bull, who fed on human flesh. It is supposed that the legend has some connection with the complex ground plan of the Minoan 'palaces' on *Crete*, such as Knossos. The origin of the Greek word is unknown: Lydian or Egyptian roots have been suggested. *Labyrinth* has been used in English since the mid-sixteenth century.

Laconia *Laconia* was the Roman name for the Greek district of *Laconica*, in the south-east of the Peleponnesus. The chief town was *Lacadaemon*, otherwise known as *Sparta*. The Spartans were noted for, amongst other characteristics, their tight-lipped brevity of speech. On one occasion, Philip of Macedonia threatened to invade *Sparta*, and sent a message: 'If I enter *Laconica*, I will level *Sparta* to the ground'. The *Spartan* leaders replied with the single word: 'If'. *Laconic*, meaning terse, has been used in English since the sixteenth century.

Lambeth Degrees, such as Doctor of Music or Doctor of Divinity, awarded by the Archbishop of Canterbury are called *Lambeth degrees*, from *Lambeth Palace*, the Archbishop's *London* house.

Landau A *landau* is a four-wheeled carriage, used today in royal processions. It has a folding top in two halves, so that it may be closed, or half-opened, or, in fine weather, opened completely. The name, sometimes spelt *lando*, comes from the Bavarian town of *Landau*, near Karlsruhe, where carriages of this pattern were first produced in the eighteenth century. A *landaulet* or *landaulette* is either a small *landau* or, from about 1900 onward, a motor-car of a particular pattern: with a closed body, the back part of which could be folded open, in the manner of a *landau*.

Laon *Lawn* is fine linen, resembling *cambric*. The word has been in use since the early fifteenth century, spelt *laune, lan* or *laun*. It comes from the French town of *Laon*, near Rheims, a place that still presents pronunciation difficulties to the English. For at least two centuries, this fine material has been used for the sleeves of bishop's surplices, so that the word can be used to describe the office of a bishop; an example of this use is in a line of Alexander Pope's: 'A Saint in Crepe is twice a Saint in Lawn'.

Latakia Properly, *Latakia* is fine 'Turkish' tobacco produced near and shipped from the Syrian port of *Latakia*, otherwise *Lattaquie* or *El Ladhiqiya*; but in practice it is any tobacco which approximates to this type.

Lebanon *Cedar of Lebanon (Cedrus libani)* were introduced to Britain, from their native *Lebanese* mountains in the seventeenth century, but were not commonly planted until about 1760.

Leghorn The Italian port of *Livorno* was, in the sixteenth and seventeenth centuries, known as *Legorno*, and was consequently dubbed *Leghorn* by British sailors, and is indeed still called *Leghorn* on some English maps. A *Leghorn hat* is so called because it is made from *Leghorn straw*, which comes from a particular type of Tuscan wheat, and was exported from *Livorno*. *Leghorns* are a well-known breed of domestic fowl.

Leicestershire The county of *Leicestershire* was famous for sheep-rearing. As well as the *Dishley Leicester*, the *Border Leicester* and the *Blue-faced Leicester* are also from *Leicestershire*.

Lesbos The connection between femal homosexual love-affairs and the Greek island of *Lesbos* is problematical. Sappho (born ca 612 BC) was the greatest female poet of the ancient world. Much of her life was spent at Mytilene, on *Lesbos*. There she was the centre of a group of female pupils and admirers, dedicated to the cult of Aphrodite, the goddess of love, beauty and reproduction. Many of Sappho's poems are enthusiastically amorous. Conjecture has taken these facts

46

to mean that *lesbianism*, or Sapphism, as the Victorians sometimes put it, flourished on *Lesbos* in those days.

Levant   To *levant* is to abscond, especially with betting or gambling losses unhonoured. There are two possible derivations. The word may come from the Spanish *levantar el campo*, which means 'to strike camp' or 'to decamp'. On the other hand, it may have the connotation of leaving for the *Levant*, the Eastern Mediterranean, which was, or was thought to be, a favourite resort of fleeing swindlers. The verb is first recorded in use in Britain in 1760.

Lido   A *lido* is a bathing beach, or a public open-air swimming pool, such as the Lansbury *Lido* in Hyde Park, *London*. All take their name from the Venetian *lido*, the sand-spit which protects *Venice* from the Adriatic. The Italian word, and *litus*, its Latin origin, mean 'the shore'.

Lille   For many generations, schoolgirls detested the stockings they were made to wear, of *lisle* thread. The word comes from the city of *Lille*, in northern *France*, where the hard, twisted cotton thread was first devised.

Lilliput (F)   When Jonathan Swift (1667-1745) published *Gulliver's Travels* in 1726, he included the imaginary country of *Lilliput*, where people were six inches in height. '*Lilliputian*' has been a synonym for diminutive since the early eighteenth century.

Lima   Sometimes called butter beans, *Lima beans (phaseolus lunatus)*, which are flat green beans, take their name from the capital of Peru, where they were cultivated very early. They were also grown in North America before the arrival of Europeans.

Limerick   Verses in *Limerick* form have often been written. The nursery-rhyme 'Hickory-dickory-dock' is probably the earliest example, and humorous verses in the familiar five-line form appeared in chap-books in the 1820s. It was not until the 1890s that the verses came to be called *limericks*. This came about because it became customary to sing a refrain, 'Will you come up to Limerick', between the comic verses that were being sung, recited or extemporized at convivial gatherings such as smoking parties. Many such verses were improper and by no means all were witty. Attempts have been made to connect the word with Edward Lear, notably by Father Matthew Russell in the *Irish Monthly*, February 1898, who claimed that *limerick* derived from *learic*. It is true that Lear employed the *limerick* form in his *Book of Nonsense*, published in 1846, as in:

A fly and a flea in a flue
Were imprisoned, so what could they do?
Said the flea, 'Let us fly'
Said the fly, 'Let us flee'
So they flew through a flaw in the flue.

Nevertheless, Edward Lear did not invent the *limerick*; the *Oxford English Dictionary* is no doubt right when it describes the supposed connection as erroneous. The *limerick* is peculiar to the English language.

Limone (S) It is tempting to assume that *lemons* derive from the town of *Limone* (*lemon* in Italian) on Lake Garda, especially as they grow there. In fact *lemon* comes from an Arabic word laimun.

Limousine Around the turn of the century, the word was coined to describe the first motor-cars with closed bodies, the earliest cars being either open, or with collapsible tops. The word was taken from the French word for a closed carriage, which in turn derives from the type of hood once worn in the old province of *Limousine*. Today, in the shortened form of *limo*, the word is used for large cars or minibuses used especially for taking passengers to airports.

Lincoln *Lincoln green*, customarily associated with Robin Hood, is not so much a colour as a bright green cloth originally made in the city of *Lincoln*. The *Lincoln* breed of sheep is the largest and heaviest British breed.

Lippiza The famous *Lippizaner* breed of horses, whose ability in *dressage* can be seen in the Spanish Riding School in *Vienna* take their name from *Lippiza*, near Trieste (now in *Italy*) where the Imperial Austrian Stud was established in 1580.

48

Lobby To *lobby* is to seek to influence somebody about a future decision. The verb derives from the ancient right of the British citizen to interview his Member of Parliament; in the House of Commons, this is usually done in the large, lofty and central *Lobby*.

Lombardy *Lombardy poplars* are prevalent in the *Lombardy* plain, in northern *Italy*. Houses used to have *lumber-rooms*, full of things stored away. *Lumber* came from an obsolete French word for pawnbroker, which in turn derived from *Lombard*, signifying a banker: both these tradesmen stored things away professionally. The *Lombards* had invented banking, a fact indicated by the name of the City of *London's* premier banking thoroughfare: *Lombard Street*. It is not known how untreated timber came to be called lumber; *lumberjack* is therefore of unknown etymological origin.

London *London clay* is a geological formation of south-east *England*. *London smoke*, *London ivy* and *London particular* all describe the dense smog which sometimes enshrouded the city in the days when cooking and heating were both done with coal fires. The stately *London plane* tree is a familiar sight in the city. *Saxifraga umbrosa*, which has pretty pink flowers on long stalks, is called *London pride*. The *London Group* was a Post-Impressionist group of British artists, which included members of the *Camden Town* group, Paul Nash (1889-1946) and Duncan Grant (1885-1978).

Lovat *Lovat*, a place in Highland Region, has given its name to a muted green colour, used for tweed suits or other garments of this shade.

Lydd Invented in the 1880s, *lyddite* is a high explosive, largely picric acid, which was first tested on the artillery ranges at *Lydd*, in Kent.

Lyons When double skirts were fashionable, in the 1860s, velvet straps were used to loop up the overskirt in three or four places for walking; these were known as *Lyons loops*.

M

Macassar   The *antimacassar* was once to be seen in innumerable Victorian parlours, protecting the upholstery of the backs of chairs from oiled hair. Often made from crochetwork, *antimacassars* date from the 1850s. The name comes from the name of the first hair-oil, *Macassar oil*, which in turn came from the port of *Macassar,* now Ujung Padang, in the Celebes, Indonesia. Paper versions of the *antimacassar* can still be encountered in first-class railway carriages, in aeroplanes and in coaches.

Macedonia   A *macédoine* is a mixture of fruits (or of vegetables) embedded in jelly. The word is French for *Macedonia*; it is said to have been applied to the dish because the *Macedonian* Empire of Alexander the Great was a miscellaneous mixture or hotch-potch.

Madison Avenue   The mid-town stretch of this *New York* City thoroughfare houses many advertising agencies; *Madison Avenue* has become synonymous with the American advertising industry.

Mafeking   *Mafficking* was a journalist's joke-word used to describe extravagant and boisterous celebration of an event. It derived from the absurd and hysterical enthusiasm of Londoners during the Boer War, when news of the raising of the siege of *Mafeking* reached *London* on 18 May 1900. *Mafeking*, on the northern border of Cape Province had been besieged by Boer forces for 217 days. The episode brought Robert Baden-Powell into prominence. Although his conduct of the defence has been questioned by modern commentators, the public impact made at the time was immense; his fame greatly helped him launch the Scout movement in 1908.

Magenta   During the Franco-Austrian War of 1859, French and Sardinian troops under the command of Marshal MacMahon defeated the Austrian forces in a fierce and bloody battle at *Magenta,* some 15 miles west of *Milan.* The action compelled the Austrians to give up *Lombardy.* This event immediately preceded the discovery of the brilliant red aniline dye, derived from coal-tar, which was named *magenta*

o commemorate the battle. This was the first chemical dye
o be used for dress material.

Magnesia   Since electro-magnetism was discovered in 1819,
magnets have had their peculiar properties imparted to them
electrically. Before this, *magnets* were made from natural
lodestone or *magnetite*; the use of this had been known
from at least as far back as the time of Thales of Miletus
(640-546 BC). *Magnetite*, or oxide of iron, was plentiful
around the ancient city of *Magnesia* in Ionia, and it is from
Magnesia that the word *magnet* derives. *Magnesia* today is
Manisa, in western *Turkey*, some 40 miles north-east of
Izmir (formerly Smyrna). The chemical element *magnesium*
(Mg), with *magnesia*, and therefore *milk of magnesia*, also
all derive from the same place.

Mahon   In Spanish, *mayonnaise* is *salsa mahonesa*, sauce of
Port Mahon and it is at or near *Mahon*, in Minorca that it
was invented. The French hold that it was invented during
the Seven Years War by the Duke of Richelieu's chef in an
effort to make local food more palatable. The Minorcans
hold that it was invented at a farmhouse where the duke had
stopped for a meal; when his chef complained that there was
nothing to make a sauce from, the farmer's wife produced
the local *salsa*, made from olive oil, lemon juice and yolk of
egg. *Mahon* was *Portus Magonis* in Roman times, named after
a Carthaginian admiral called *Mago*. *Mayonnaise* is therefore
the only word in the language with a Punic root.

Majorca   *Majolica* was a word first used in *Italy* in the
fourteenth century to describe lustred Spanish earthenware
imported from *Spain* via *Majorca*, then called *Majolica*.
From the mid-fifteenth century, copies were being made in
Tuscany and elsewhere in *Italy* and this too is called *Majolica*.
It is still made today: the earthenware body is coated with
tin-glaze, on which is laid and fired a painted decoration.
The name is also used for lead-glazed earthenware with oxide
coloured glazes made in *Staffordshire* in the eighteenth and
nineteenth centuries.

Malacca   *Malacca canes* are fine walking-sticks, rich brown
in colour and often clouded or mottled. Properly they should

51

be made from the stem of the *Calamus Scipionum* an
come from the *Malacca*, now *Melaka*, district on the we
coast of Malaysia.

Malmaison Both the *Malmaison rose* and the *Malmaiso
carnation* take their name from the Empress Josephine
palace of *Malmaison*, near Versailles.

Malta Many places have breeds of dog named after then
Malta is unusual, perhaps unique, in having given its name t
both dogs and cats. *Maltese cats* are a short-haired bluish-gre
breed, once very popular in the USA; *Maltese dogs* are th
most ancient breed of lap-dog, with 2000 years of histor
behind them; they have white silky hair which almost reach
the ground. There are also the world famous *Maltese lac
maltese mushrooms* and *Malta fever*, a complicated and lon
lasting afflication. *Maltese crosses* almost fill a square shap
with limbs which are very narrow at the core and graduall
expand, and indented extremities. Originally the badge of th
Knights of *Malta*, the *Maltese cross* has been adopted, i
various forms, by many well-known orders, including th
Order of Merit; both the Victoria Cross and the German Iro
Cross are *Maltese crosses*. A *Maltese cross* stitch is used fc
background-filling in embroidery.

Manhattan A *manhattan* is a cocktail of whisky, swee
vermouth and bitters. It was almost certainly invented an
named in *New York* City's *Manhattan Club* as early as th
1870s, but there is also a legend which attributes its origi
to a Maryland bartender who is said to have invented th
drink to revive a wounded duellist in the 1840s.

Manila *Manilla hemp*, or abaca, is a fibrous material of
tained from the sheathing leaves of *Musa textilis*, whic
grows in the Philippines, of which the city of *Manila* is th
capital. *Manilla hemp* is naturally buoyant and resistant t
water; ropes made from it were much used at sea and fc
rock-climbing before the days of man-made fibres. *Manil
hemp* is also used for matting, textile fabric and tough pape
especially envelopes.

Mantua *Mantua hose* were high quality early knitted sil
stockings. A *mantua* was a loose gown joined to an overski
52

ith a train. *Mantuas* were so popular from the mid-sevententh century for formal and social occasions that *mantuaaker* became synonymous with dressmaker. There is a *antua-maker's* seam. The city of *Mantua*, properly *Mantova*, in the *Lombardy* plain in northern *Italy*.

arathon   A race of 26 miles and 385 yards (42,195 metres) a *marathon*. The word is also used to describe anything ngthy or protracted: international negotiations, speeches, ourt cases and so on. The name comes from the battle of *arathon*, in *Attica* in 490 BC. Herodotus (c484-c420 BC) cords that a man called Pheidippides ran from *Athens* to oarta to secure help before the battle; a more picturesque gend claims that he ran from *Marathon* to *Athens* with the ews that the Athenians had defeated the Persians, dramatially dropping dead on arrival. It was this legend which caused commemorative race to be run from *Marathon* to *Athens* bout 20 miles) during the first modern Olympic Games, eld at *Athens* in 1896. The present distance was established the *London* Olympics of 1908, when the race started at *indsor* and ended at the White City Stadium, Shepherd's ush.

arseilles   The National Anthem of *France* is known as the *arseillaise* because it was sung by patriots from *Marseilles* as ey entered *Paris* in July 1792, and at the storming of the uileries Palace the following month. It had been written ad composed by an army officer called Rouget de Lisle urlier in 1792, with the title '*Le Chant de guerre de l'armée u Rhin*' and had been immediately successful.

artigues   A *martingale* is a piece of harness, a strap fastened the noseband to inhibit a horse from throwing up its head; *martingale-stay* is a piece of rigging, for guying down a jiboom. The word was originally used, by Rabelais amongst hers, in *chausses à la martingale*, denoting stockings or hose stened at the back; this is commonly supposed to have eant 'hose in the fashion of *Martigues*'. The ancient town of *artigues* is in the *département* of Bouches-du-Rhône, some 3 miles north-west of *Marseilles*.

Masovia   A *mazurka* is a dance in 3/4 time with the emphasis on the second beat. It comes from the Polish province of *Masovia*, in which Warsaw (Warszawa) is situated. Originally a folk dance it was introduced into court circles in the late eighteenth century. It spread to western Europe generally in the early nineteenth century.

Meander   To *meander* is to wind about sinuously, to turn to and fro: hence to wander aimlessly. The word comes from the river in western *Turkey* now called the *Buyuk Menderes*. In classical times this was the river *Meander*, which does indeed pursue a very sinuous course for part of its length. If a house is named 'Meander', it is most likely not because of a holiday in *Turkey*, but is a constructed pun or joke-name 'Me-and-'er'.

Mecca   All Muslims want to make, at some time in their lives, the pilgrimage, called the *haj*, to the holy cities of Medina and *Mecca*, in Saudi Arabia and thousands do so every year. *Mecca (Umm-al-qura*, the mother of cities in Arabic) is Mohammed's birthplace; it has immensely powerful human magnetic qualities, so that the word is used generally to describe a place that people long to visit, the birthplace of a cult, a faith or even the main centre of a pastime or sport.

Meissen   Porcelain was made in the town of *Meissen*, some 15 miles from *Dresden*, in East *Germany*, after a way of copying Chinese porcelain had been discovered (by J. F Bottger) in 1710. It was known in Britain as *Dresden* china.

Melton Mowbray   *Melton* is a kind of broadcloth, used for hunting jackets, called *melton jackets*, and named after the fox-hunting centre of *Melton Mowbray, Leicestershire*. There was also a *melton pad*, a species of hernia truss adapted for use on horseback; *meltonian cream* was originally devised for polishing hunting boots. *Melton Mowbray* is also noted for its pork pies.

Mendlesham   A *Mendlesham chair* or *Suffolk chair* is a low-backed nineteenth century variant of the *Windsor* *hair*, with a square-cut back. It takes the name of the *Suffolk* village where it was no doubt invented or devised.

Milan   When the word was first used, as in Henry VIII's Privy Purse accounts for 1530, *milliner*, a corruption of *Milaner*, meant a seller of 'fancy apparel', especially of *Milanese* manufacture, *Milan* bonnets, ribbons, gloves and other female accessories. Later *milliner* came to mean a maker of women's hats and *millinery* to mean women's hats and their trimming. Properly, of course, the place is *Milano*.

Monemvasia   Richard III's brother the Duke of Clarence is always said to have met his death by being drowned in a butt of *malmsey* wine. The wine originally came from *Monemvasia,* in *Greece*, a word which became *malmasia* in medieval Latin, and *malmsey* in English. The same type of wine came to be made in *Italy, Spain* and Madeira.

Monmouth   *Monmouth caps*: simple knitted hats with tall crowns and no brims were popular with Welshmen, sailors and soldiers in the late sixteenth century.

Monte Carlo   Shoes with two-coloured uppers, for men, were no doubt thought to be raffish, if not downright caddish when they were nick-named 'co-respondent shoes'. Their other name is even more evocative: *Monte Carlo trollers*, a phrase dating from the 1920s.

Monterey   The *Monterey pine (Pinus radiata)* is native to a very small area of wet winters and hot dry summers in the *Monterey* Peninsula, California. It was introduced to Britain in 1833.

Montilla   *Amontillado* was formerly a wine of the *sherry* type produced in *Montilla*. The word has come to mean a matured *sherry* in which the 'flor' has developed, dry and deep gold in colour. *Montilla* lies in the hilly country south of the city of *Cordoba*.

Morocco   Leather made from *Moroccan* goatskin, tanned with sumac, was called *morocco*. Other mediterranean states took to exporting similar leather so that some curious wording, such as *French morocco*, was used. *Morocco* is still used for bookbinding and for upholstery.

Mortella, Cape *Martello towers* are anti-Napoleonic defence works built on the coast of south-east *England* in the early 1800s. The name comes from *Corsica*, where a small round tower at *Cape Mortella* had been captured by the Mediterranean Fleet under Lord Hood in 1794, after a spirited defence by a small party of men. The design of this small fortress, and its ability to withstand the fleet's cannonade made a great impression. The design was adapted for use in the forts which can still be seen in *Suffolk, Essex,* Kent and Sussex. *Mortella* means wild myrtle in Italian.

Mortlake *Mortlake tapestries* were made, during the reigns of James I and Charles I in the *Surrey* town of *Mortlake*, the finishing point of the *Oxford* and *Cambridge* Boat Race.

Moscow The cocktail known as a *Moscow mule* (vodka, ginger beer with lime or lemon juice) was first mixed in 1948 by the owner of the Cock 'n Bull Tavern in Los Angeles: Jack Morgan. In the 1870s, *Moscow wrappers* were fashionable; these were loose, full overcoats for both sexes.

Mosul The finely-woven cotton fabric, *muslin*, first came from the city of *Mosul (Al Maursil)* in northern Iraq. *Muslin* is now manufactured universally. The Italian word for *muslin* is *mussolino*.

Musselburgh It is curious that very few toponyms have found their way into the colourful language of golf. *Musselburgh scoot* is one of them, describing a particular type of approach shot. Whether it was in fact practised at the Royal *Musselburgh* Golf Club, or is merely said to have been, is not known.

N

Nanjing *Nanjing* is the chief city of the Jiangsu province of *China*. Previously known as *Nanking*, it was once a place from which naturally yellow cotton was exported. This was called *nankeen*, and was often used for making trousers, known as *nankeens*.

Neanderthal *Neanderthal man* is a type of primitive man, named after the discoveries made, in 1859, at *Neanderthal*, then in *Prussia*.

Nelson *Nelsons* and *half-nelsons* are wrestling holds. Their origin is not certain, but it is extremely likely that the words come from the Lancashire town of *Nelson*.

Newcastle upon Tyne 'To carry coals to *Newcastle*' is to do something totally unnecessary. The *Newcastle* and *Durham* coal fields were the best known in England, supplying the *London* area from the earliest days of the coal industry. Coal towns named *Newcastle* after *Newcastle upon Tyne* are to be found in South Africa, Australia and New Zealand. *Newcastle disease* is a highly contagious viral disease of chickens and other domestic and wild birds, otherwise known as fowl-pest. It was first recorded in *Newcastle upon Tyne* in 1926.

Newgate A *Newgate Calendar* is a record of criminal activity, named after the famous *Newgate Prison* which once stood in the City of *London*. A *Newgate fringe* or *frill* comes from the same source; this is a beard grown below the jaw-line on an otherwise clean-shaven face, simulating a hangman's noose.

Newmarket The *Newmarket coat*, dating from the late 1830s, was a tail coat with the front sloping away from above waist level, for riding. Later called the 'cutaway' it is the ancestor of the morning coat, still worn today on formal occasions. At one time there was a *Newmarket jacket*, hip-length with flapped pockets, for women. A *Newmarket vest* is a waistcoat of plaid or check pattern, buttoned high. All these, with the well-known card game of *Newmarket*, take their name from the racing headquarters on the *Suffolk-Cambridgeshire* border.

New Orleans   The *New Orleans* style of jazz has an early and honoured place in the history of the music. It was in *New Orleans* that jazz evolved as the standard form of entertainment in sporting and gambling houses; and it was from *New Orleans* that jazz spread, initially up the Mississippi, to *Kansas City* and to *Chicago*. The *New Orleans* style was revived in the 1950s when it was known as 'trad'.

New York   *New York City* and *New York State* have given their name to many things. Wild life includes the *New York Warbler*, the *New York Weasel* and *New York Bats*, which have heads shaped like those of mice. There is the *New York Shield-fern (Dryopteris noveboracensis)*. Most interesting of all is the *New York Gloria Mundi*; this is a very large apple, and accounts for the otherwise mysterious nickname for *New York City*: 'The Big Apple'.

Nicaea   The *Nicene Creed* is based on that adopted at the first ecumenical Council at *Nicaea*, in the year 325. The place is now the Turkish city of Iznik.

Nîmes   *Denim* is short for *serge de Nîmes*. This was a kind of serge made at *Nîmes,* in southern *France;* called *serge de Nim*, it was known in Britain from the seventeenth century. Later the same word was used, at first in *America*, for the familiar twilled cotton material in universal use today.

Norfolk   There are *Norfolk dumplings* (made from bread dough), *Norfolk turkeys, Norfolk plovers*, and *Norfolk capons* (red herrings). The common reed used for thatching is the *Norfolk reed* (Phragmitis australis). *Norfolk jackets* are belted, pleated and usually tweed; *Norfolk suits* are *Norfolk jackets* with matching breeches. *Norfolk Howards* are bugs; they are so called from an announcement in *The Times* on 26 June 1862 stating that Joseph Bug, of *Norfolk* had assumed the surname of Howard. *Norfolk spaniels* was an early name for English springer spaniels; *Norfolk terriers* are drop-eared versions of *Norwich terriers*. But the *Norfolk pine (Araucaria heterophylla)* has nothing to do with the English county; it is native to *Norfolk Island*, about 500 miles north-west of New Zealand.

58

Norway It is no surprise to learn that the well-wooded country of *Norway* has given its name to the *Norway birch, fir, spruce, maple* and *pine*. There are *Norway rats, Norway haddock, Norway crows* and *Norway lobsters*, although the latter are also called *Dublin Bay prawns*. There are *Norway neckcloths, Norway ragstone, Norway skiffs* and *Norway yawls*.

Norwich Materials to which the city of *Norwich* gave its name include *Norwich crepe, Norwich damask* and *Norwich poplin*; and there are *Norwich shawls*. The *Norwich School* is the best known of the English regional schools of painters; it flourished in the first decades of the nineteenth century, its leading figures being John Crome (1768-1821) and John Sell Cotman (1782-1824). *Norwich terriers* are easily distinguished from *Norfolk terriers*, which they otherwise resemble, by their ears, which stick up in the same style as *Norwich* Cathedral spire.

Nottingham *Nottingham ale* used to be regarded as especially powerful. *Nottingham white* is an obselete term for white lead. There is a *Nottingham style* of coarse fishing. There are *Nottingham stoneware, Nottingham brickwork* and pale creamy-grey *Nottingham stone*. *Nottingham drill* is a material, and the machine-made *Nottingham lace* is well-known. *Nottingham catchfly* is a white-flowered perennial herb (*silene mutaris*). In cricket, the *Nottingham foward cut* is made with the left leg well forward. The city was also the place of origin of the *Nottingham One-Club* bridge bidding convention.

O

Oatland The *Oatland village hat*, a straw hat for country wear, took its name from the place where the Duchess of York (1767-1840) lived in the 1800s. Her husband is immortalised in the nursery rhyme 'The Grand Old Duke of York'.

Oerlikon The *Oerlikon* gun, much used in the Royal Navy in World War II, was a light quick-firing anti-aircraft weapon. It had been developed by the Swiss firm of *Werkzeugmaschinenfabrik Oerlikon Buhrle* in the Zurich suburb of *Oerlikon*.

Olympia There were many places in ancient *Greece* where annual competitive games were held. The most famous of these were held at *Olympia*. Some of the architectural remains there date from the thirteenth century BC; the first definite reference to the games at *Olympia* is of 776 BC. It was an imitation of these games that the modern *Olympic Games* were started.

Olympus, Mount There are several mountains in *Greece* called *Olympus*. The most famous is the high (nearly 3000 m) range on the borders of Thessaly and *Macedonia*. This is the place where the top of the mountains was thought to be the home of the gods of the ancient world. *Olympian* accordingly means celestial, magnificent, condescending or superior.

Orange The Dutch Royal Family is *The House of Orange*. The town of this name, about 13 miles north of Avignon, in the Rhône valley, once gave its name to a small principality, which was inherited by *Prince William of Orange-Nassau* in 1544; this was William the Silent, who was assassinated in 1584. It was his great-grandson William III of Great Britain who was active in Ireland during his reign, and gave his name to the *Orange Order*. The principality of *Orange* was given up to *France* under the Treaty of Utrecht in 1713.

Oranges, however, are spurious toponyms: this sense of the word comes from the Sanskrit *naranga*.

Osborne *Osborne biscuits,* which are plain and sweet, were first made in 1860. The manufacturers wanted to call them Victoria biscuits, but Queen Victoria would not allow this, and suggested the name of her favourite residence instead. The Queen and the Prince Consort had bought the *Osborne* estate, on the Isle of Wight, as a seaside holiday retreat in 1845.

Ottoman Empire An *ottoman* is an armless and backless sofa, usually with a hinged seat and solid sides, for storage. They were popular pieces of furniture in Victorian days and took their name from the *Ottoman,* or Turkish *Empire,* where these seats were first used. *Ottoman cloth* is a dress-fabric of a warp-ribbed structure and made from hard crisp yarn. The *Ottoman Empire* got its name from *Ottoman,* or *Othman I,* Sultan at the beginning of the fourteeenth century. It is curious that divan, another type of sofa, though not a toponym, also came from the *Ottoman Empire,* where the Privy Council, and its Chamber, were both called the divan.

Oxford The University city of *Oxford* has given its name to a very large lists of things. There is *Oxford clay,* which is dark blue in colour. *Oxford corners* are used in printing, *Oxford hollows* in book-binding. *Oxford* has its own shade of dark *blue.* There is supposed to be an *Oxford accent,* in speech. *Oxford ragwort* has the intriguing Latin name of *Senecio squalidus. Oxford bags* were especially broad-bottomed, or flared, trousers. *Oxfords* are a style of shoes; *Oxford button-overs* are *Oxfords* with buttons instead of laces. *Oxford ties* are neckties of uniform width. There is an *Oxford* breed of sheep.

P

Padua A *pavan* is a grave and stately dance, introduced to Britain in the sixteenth century. The word comes from the Italian *danza Padovana* 'dance of *Padua*'.

Paisley Shawls, made for over 200 years at *Paisley* in Strathclyde near Glasgow, had their own curvilinear patterns, known as *Paisley patterns*, still popular today.

Palatine All *palaces* take their name from the first of their kind, which was the combination of government centre and living quarters built on the *Palatine Hill* by the Emperor Augustus (63 BC − AD 14).

Pale The expression 'beyond *the pale*' comes from *The English Pale*. For centuries after Ireland was conquered by Henry II, *The English Pale* was the part of the island where English law and dominion were acknowledged. Over the years the extent of this area varied, but it always included Kildare, Louth, Meath and Dublin. The expression ceased to have any meaning in Elizabethan times, when it was extended to the whole island. There was a similar *Pale* around Calais. The word's root is the same as that for *paling* and *palisade*.

Palm Beach A lightweight fabric, and the suits made from it, were both called *Palm Beach*, from the fashionable but very warm Florida resort.

Panama *Panama hat* is almost a misnomer. They were first made in Ecuador, but were much worn in and distributed around the world from *Panama*, from the middle of the nineteenth century. The *Panama hat palm (Carludovica palmata)* produced the leaves from which the hats are made. There are also *Panama fever*, and *Panama disease*, which affects banana trees.

Paris For centuries the centre of fashion, it is not surprising that most of the *Paris* toponyms are connected with clothes. There are *Paris cloth, Paris cut, Paris felt, Paris net, Paris embroidery, Paris green* and many others. There is the *Paris daisy*, or marguerite. *Plaster of Paris* is so called because the fine white plaster of which it is made was obtained from gypsum from the Montmartre district of *Paris*.

Parma   There are both *pearmain apples* and *pears*. The word *pearmain* comes from the Latin *parmensis* 'of *Parma*'. *Parmesan* means the same in French and refers especially to the hard *Parmesan cheese*, especially favoured for grating and cooking and made in the *Parma* district of north *Italy* for over 900 years. Hard cheese is of course made in other parts of *Italy*. *Parma ham*, uncooked smoked ham, called *prosciutto* in *Italy* does not necessarily come from anywhere near the city of *Parma*.

Pembroke   *Pembroke tables* have four fixed legs, with two flaps supported by two additional legs fixed to the main structure. First devised and made in *Pembroke*, the earliest examples date from the 1750s.

Penang   The term *Penang lawyer* is, or perhaps was, Royal Navy slang for a cane. The best canes come from the east, particularly from Malaysia.

Pentagon   *The Pentagon* is a huge five-sided Washington building, put up by the United States Army during World War II. It now houses the US Defense Department, and is often given a voice of its own by the media: '*The Pentagon* views the situation . . .' for example, when reporting Defense Department thinking.

Perche, La   The powerful breed of working horse, the most famous French heavy horse, called *Percheron*, was first bred in La Perche, a region which lies between Normandy and Orléans. *La Perche* was an independent fief until annexed to the French crown in 1483.

Pergamon   *Parchment* is a sheepskin or goatskin prepared for writing; the word comes from the French *parchemin*, which in turn came from the Latin *pergamena*, 'of *Pergamum*'. This was the ancient Greek city of *Pergamon*, famous for its learning and library. *Parchment* was developed there when one of the Ptolomys introduced very early economic sanctions and refused supplies of papyrus, the alternative writing substance, from *Egypt*. *Pergamon* is now *Bergama*, in *Turkey*.

Persia The word *peach* comes, of course, from the French *pêche*. That word came from the Latin *persicum malum*, meaning 'Persian apple'. The tree from which this delectable fruit comes is *Amygdalus persica*.

Phasis The word *pheasant* goes back to the Greek *phasianos*, the *Phasian bird*. This refers to the city, river and district of *Phasis*, in the classical Colchis, now the Caucasus, at the eastern end of the Black Sea.

Philistia The use of the word *Philistine* in its modern sense — a materialistic person uninterested in art and culture — was begun, in the 1860s by Matthew Arnold (1822-88). He took it from German universities, where *philister* was then slang for non-students, or outsiders. The Old Testament *Philistines*, a warlike people of uncertain origins who constantly harassed the Israelites were, to the latter, also outsiders. *Philistia* is today part of Israel.

Phrygia A *frieze* is a band of painted or sculptured decoration. As an order of architecture a *frieze* is a horizontal band between an architrave and a cornice, characteristic of buildings in ancient *Phrygia*, today part of *Turkey*.

Piccadilly Long combed-out whiskers were fashionable in the 1870s and 1880s. They were called *Piccadilly weepers*, from the London street where men of fashion used then to stroll.

Pilsen *Pilsen beer*, or *pilsener*, is sometimes thought to be German beer. In fact it gets its name from the city and province of *Pilsen*, in Czechoslovakia, (also known as Plzen) where the pale lager beer originated.

Pistoia There is no complete agreement amongst etymologists about the word *pistol*. One theory traces the origin thus: *pistol* (English), *pistole/pistolet* (French), *pistoletto/pistolese* (Italian), the last word in this chain meaning 'of *Pistoia*' a province and city about 35 miles north-west of
64

Florence. Pistolet also meant a small dagger, and some gold coins were known, in the sixteenth century, as *pistolets*; the word is still in use in Belgium for a small bread roll.

Plymouth *Plymouth gin*, once the favourite tipple of officers in the Royal Navy, was originally made in the city in imitation of *Hollands*. *Plymouth pottery* was the first English hard-paste porcelain, dating from 1768. The religious body, *Plymouth Brethren*, was founded in *Plymouth* in 1830. *Plymouth rock* are large, grey black-striped fowl from *America*, taking their name from the landing place of those who sailed from *Plymouth* in the *Mayflower* in 1620. *Plymouth cloak* is an obscure seventeenth century slang expression for a cudgel.

Poland It is not certain that the word *polka* came from *Poland*; half-steps are used in the dance, and *polka* may derive from *pulka*, the Czech word for half. What is certain is that the dance swept through Europe like an epidemic, reaching *Paris* in 1840 and *London* in the spring of 1842. It was popular and fashionable, and the word was used at the time by many manufacturers of clothes. *Polka-dots* survive today. A *Polonaise* is a dance introduced into the Polish court in the seventeenth century, a stately and intricate promenade in couples. *Polonaise* is also cloth, a silk or cotton mixture. A *polonaise* is also a dress with an over-skirt bunched up behind, popular for 100 years from about 1770. *Polish boots* were popular with women in the 1860s, having tassels and coloured heels. *Polish greatcoats,* worn by men with evening dress throughout the nineteenth century, were long, with fur collars, cuffs and lapels.

Pontefract The liquorice-based *Pomfret cake* takes its name from the *Yorkshire* town where it first became known, but prefers the early name of *Pomfret*, derived from the Anglo-Norman *Pont fret*, rather than the Latinized *Pontefract*. Both the names, of course, mean the same thing: 'broken bridge'.

Portland *Portland stone* is valuable building limestone quarried at *Portland Bill* in Dorset. *Portland cement* is not made there, but takes the name because it is a similar colour to *Portland stone*.

Porto *Port* is short for *Oporto wine*. The term has been used since the seventeenth century for the fortified wine which evolved in the *Porto* district of *Portugal* and is exported from the Portugese city of *Porto*, known to the British as *Oporto*. *O porto* means 'the port' in Portuguese.

Portugal When the *Portuguese* navy was past its prime, small sea-creatures with a powerful sting were given the derisive name of *Portuguese men-of-war*. In the late seventeenth century, chairs and side-tables were sometimes made with turned and shapely *Portuguese legs*. *Portuguese border stitch* is a surface embroidery stitch used for stems and marginal lines.

Prémontré The *Premonstratensian* order of Canons Regular was founded in 1119 at *Prémontré*, near *Laon*, in northern *France*. The first English Premonstratensian house was established, at Newsham, Lincolnshire little more than twenty years later.

Prussia *Prussian blue* is well named; the colour was discovered, by accident, in *Berlin*, in 1704. *Prussic acid* (hydrocyanic acid) was obtained from *Prussian blue* pigment. *Prusse*, French for *Prussian*, gives us *spruce*. Imports from the Hanseatic towns on the *Prussian* coast — beer, timber, canvas, leather — were called *spruce*; the *spruce tree* got its name in this fashion. 'To *spruce* oneself up' originally meant to dress in *spruce leather* clothing.

Q

Quai d'Orsay   French foreign policy is sometimes attributed, by a process called metonomy, to the *Paris* street in which the Ministry of Foreign Affairs stands. The street is named after a General, Count d'Orsay, whose second son, Alfred, Count d'Orsay (1801-1852) was the famous dandy who lived in *London* in the 1830s and 1840s.

R

Ragusa   *Argosies,* such as the vessels which play an important part in the plot of *The Merchant of Venice,* were originall large carracks or trading ships built at *Ragusa,* in *Dalmatic* The word was first anglicized as *Arragosa.* Later, the wor went on to mean a substantial merchant ship, whereve built. *Ragusa* today is Dubrovnik, in Yugoslavia.

Ramillies   Worn in the eighteenth century by Guard officers, *Ramillies wigs* had long tapered queues, plaite and tied with bows. The name came from the Battle c *Ramillies,* Marlborough's great victory in 1706.

Rhode Island   The small East Coast State of *Rhode Islan* has given its name to an apple, the *Rhode Island greening* to a type of grass, the *Rhode Island bent*; and also to th *Rhode Island* domestic fowl, of which there are two kinds the brownish-red *Rhode Island Red* and the *Rhode Islan White.*

Rockaway   A *rockaway* is a four-wheeled American pleasur carriage, open at the sides, with two or three seats and standing top. Carriages of this pattern were first made a *Rockaway,* New Jersey in the mid-nineteenth century.

Rome   The first printing types, in *Germany,* were heav gothic letters. *Roman* is short for *Roman type* copied fror the elegant letters on Latin inscriptions from the *Roma* world. Printers also use *roman* to distinguish upright (*roman* characters from sloped (*italic*) letters. The city of *Rome* ha given its name to a long list: *Roman law, Roman pottery Roman noses, Roman fever, Roman apricots, Roman beans Roman pigeons,* and the *Roman balance,* an early weighin machine. There are the fireworks called *roman candles,* th name also being Army slang for *Roman Catholics.*

Roscommon   The *Roscommon* breed of sheep is the onl pure Irish breed. The County of *Roscommon* is in the centr of Ireland.

Rose Hill   The *Rosella (Platycercus eximius)* is a beautifu Australian parakeet, which gets its charming name from *Ros*

ill, the residence at Parramatta near Sydney, of the Governor
f New South Wales.

ubicon   To cross the *Rubicon* is to take a decisive and
revocable step. The *Rubicon* was a river which formed the
oundary between the Roman republic and the province of
is-alpine Gaul. When Julius Caesar crossed the *Rubicon* in
9 BC with his legions he was in fact opening a civil war.
: is thought that the river concerned is that now called the
iumicino, which flows into the Adriatic a few miles north-
est of Rimini. There is a card game called *Rubicon bezique.*

ugby   In late-Victorian days undergraduates at, say, *Oxford*
ad their own *argot* in which breakfast became brekker, a
cture a lecker, and a waste-paper-basket a wagger-pagger-
agger. In this tribal language, the two codes of football in
se at the University naturally became soccer (or socker) for
ssociation, and *rugger,* for *rugby.* The latter game had been
vented in 1823 at *Rugby* School.

uritania (F)   Anthony Hope Hawkins (1863-1933), who used
nly the first two of his names as his pen name published
he Prisoner of Zenda in 1894. Both this book and its
uccessor *Rupert of Hentzau,* published in 1898, were
mmensely successful and were set in an imaginary Central
uropean country, small, beautiful, feudal and romantic.
e called this place *Ruritania*; the books made a powerful
npression and the word *Ruritanian* has often been used to
escribe a court romance, a petty state or an intrigue.

ussia   The list of *Russian* toponyms reflects the size of
e country. There are *Russian bears,* and cats called *Russian
lues.* There is a *Russian poplar* tree, a *Russian thistle,* native
 America, and the fast-growing and very prolific climber
ussian vine (Polygonum baldschanicum). In embroidery
ere are *Russian overcast* and *Russian drawn filling,* often
sed together to form a pattern. There is a game of patience
illed *Russian banker,* and there is *Russian bagatelle. Russian
garettes* are small and have filter-holders. There is *Russian
lad. Russian dolls* are wooden, painted and hollow, with

progressively smaller dolls inside. *Russian roulette* is a des
perate form of bravado, where one bullet is loaded in a six
chamber revolver, the revolver spun and then fired at one'
own head.

S

St Joachimsthal   Silver *dollars* were first issued in the USA in 1794, after earlier legislation. The word is traced back, through the Dutch *daler* to the sixteenth century German coin, the *thaler*. *Thalers* were first struck in the *thal* (valley) of *St Joachimsthal*, in *Bohemia* in 1519, where a silver mine had started operation three years earlier.

Samaria   Anyone who lends a helping hand is a *Samaritan*. The name comes from the district of *Samaria* in the Holy Land, and the expression originates with the story of the compassionate *Samaritan* in St Luke 10: 30-37. *The Samaritans,* started in the City of *London*, are now a worldwide caring organization who do most of their work via the telephone.

Samos   *Samian ware* is the famous red-glazed pottery mass-produced in *France* and *Germany*, and imitated in Britain, in Roman times and used throughout the Roman Empire. The name comes from its supposed resemblance to the pottery of the Greek island of *Samos*.

Saratoga   Like a cabin-trunk, a *Saratoga trunk* was an exceptionally large and heavy trunk for carrying women's clothes. The once-fashionable *New York* State summer resort of *Saratoga Springs* provided the name; the implication was that, to go there and to keep up with those there, an enormous wardrobe was required.

Sardinia   The true *sardine, clupea pilchardus*, was prevalent off the coasts of *Brittany* and of *Sardinia*, which provided the name for the fish; but what is today packed in oil and sold as *sardines* may perhaps be something else. The word *sardonic* reached *England* in the seventeenth century, and is derived from *sardonique* (French), *sardonian* (Latin), and *sardonios* (Greek), all referring to the island of *Sardinia*. It is to the Greeks that we owe the notion that *herba sardonia*, which is to be found in the island, will, if eaten, cause grimaces like bitter laughter.

Savoy   The once substantial state of *Savoy*, between *France* and *Italy* survives in the mountainous French *département* of

71

Savoie. The *Savoy cabbage*, a rough-leaved 'variety, came from the region; there is also a *Savoy biscuit*, a kind of sponge biscuit used in making *Charlotte Russe*. A *Savoyard* is not only an inhabitant of *Savoy*: the name used to be applied to the members of the D'Oyly Carte Opera Company, who monopolized professional performance of the '*Savoy*' Operas of Gilbert and Sullivan which were first performed at the *Savoy Theatre* in *London*. The theatre and the adjacent *Savoy Hotel* were both named after the former *Savoy Palace*; the latter was named by the man who built it: Peter de Savoy, uncle of Henry III's Queen Eleanor.

Saxony   Fine wool called *Saxony* came from this German kingdom, with the various cloths made from it: *Saxony coating*, *Saxony flannel* and *Saxony cord*.

Scarborough   In the 1860s the *Scarborough hat*, for women, became very popular; it was worn with the brim turned up in front. The *Scarborough ulster* was a development of the *Ulster* coat; it had a cape and hood but no sleeves.

Schenectady   The world golfing authorities in 1919 outlawed a type of putter known as a *Schenectady putter*; it had been developed at the *Schenectady Golf Club*, in *New York* State.

Scotland   *Scotch*, a shortened form of *Scotch whisky*, is an adjective-turned-noun which can be said to have immortalized a nation. It stands alone. *Scotch mist* (fine rain) is rightly thought to be characteristic of the country. *Scotch terriers*, sometimes called *Aberdeen terriers*, like *Scotch Blackface sheep*, were bred there. There are *Scotch eggs* (boiled eggs in sausage meat) and *Scotch pancakes* (drop scones). The *Scottish baronial* style of architecture has been used all over the world with varying degrees of exuberance. Tall cranes on building sites are nicknamed *scotchmen* in tribute to generations of *Scots* engineers. The schottische is a dance which has nothing to do with *Scotland*, as it is a corrupt German word. The South African scotch cart likewise: it is an Anglicized version of the Afrikaans skotskar.

Scotland Yard *Scotland Yard* is the name of the Head-quarters of the Metropolitan Police Force. From 1829 to 1967 the headquarters was in *New Scotland Yard*, off the Thames embankment, a street which took its name from a part of the old *Whitehall Palace* on the site. When they moved to Broadway, Westminster, the police took the name *Scotland Yard* with them. For years they had been allusively known as *Scotland Yard*.

Sedan (S) The sedan chair, much used in the 17th and 18th centuries, was apparently introduced to *England* by Charles I, after a visit to *Spain*, when Prince of Wales, in 1623. Dr Johnson thought that the word came from the French city of *Sedan*, but it is more probably derived from the Latin *sedes*, a seat. In later years, in the USA, sedan meant a saloon car.

Seidlitz The water taken from a spring at *Seidlitz* in *Bohemia* has a powerful aperient effect, at it is impregnated with magnesium sulphate and carbonic acid. *Seidlitz powder*, a proprietory name, contains a mixture which, when dissolved in water, has the same properties.

Selters, Nieder *Seltzer-water*, an early form of natural soda-water, known in Britain from the mid-eighteenth century, originated from the village of *Nieder Selters*, in Hesse-Nassau, *Prussia*. Man-made soda-water was first made by Joseph Priestley in 1767. When first manufactured it was sometimes called *seltzer-water*, a name not wholly extinct even today in the USA.

Serendip *Serendipity* is the faculty of making happy and unexpected discoveries by accident. The word was invented by Horace Walpole (1717-1797), who wrote, in a letter dated 28 January 1754, of forming the word from the title of a fairy-tale, *The Three Princes of Serendip*, the heroes of which were always making discoveries by accident and sagacity of things they were not in quest of . . .' *Serendip* was an early name for the island of *Sri Lanka* (*Ceylon* before 1972).

Seville The bitter oranges from the *Seville* district of Spain (*citrus aurantium*) have, since the sixteenth century, been especially favoured for making marmalade. Olive oil from the same district is called *Seville oil.*

Sèvres   For centuries, fine and costly porcelain has been made at *Sèvres,* just outside *Paris* in the *département* of Seine-et-Oise.

Shaftesbury Avenue   There are half-a-dozen theatres in this *London* street, more than in any other single thoroughfare; *Shaftesbury Avenue,* accordingly, has become shorthand, as it were, for 'the *London* commercial theatre'.

Shandong   The soft undressed Chinese silk called *shantung* first came from the north-eastern province of *China* once called by this name, but now usually rendered as *Shandong.*

Shanghai   To *shanghai* is to make a man insensible by one means or another and to ship him on board a vessel needing hands for enforced service. The verb originated in the USA; it may describe what is thought to have been the practice in in *China's* largest port and city, or may equally well describe what once occurred on a vessel sailing to *Shanghai.*

Shangri-La (F)   In 1933 James Hilton (1900-1954) published a popular novel entitled *Lost Horizon,* in which he described an imaginary, idyllic and remote mountain kingdom in the Himalayas, calling it *Shangri-La.* Many houses have since been given the name.

Shetland   The *Shetland Islands* have their own breed of sheep. Wool spun there is *Shetland wool.* The diminutive breed of *Shetland ponies* (sometimes called *shelties*) are noted for their sure-footedness, intelligence and good nature.

Shillelagh   A *shillelagh* is an Irish cudgel. It is so called because of a famous oak wood near the village of *Shillelagh,* County Wicklow, from which the finest weapons of this sort were fashioned.

Siam   Before 1939, Thailand was called *Siam.* It was from that country that *Siamese cats* came. *Siamese twins* can of course be born anywhere. They are called *Siamese* because of the fame of the conjoined twins, named Chang and Eng, who were born in *Siam* in 1811, and who toured the world as freaks before dying in 1874.

Siena   Several related colours take their name from the Italian city of *Siena*, where there was an earthy substance — *terra di Sien(n)a* — available to create them: *siena* or *burnt siena, siena brown* and *siena drab.*

Silesia   The region of *Silesia*, in *Poland* and in Czecholovakia produced a thin and flimsy linen, which was certainly called *sleasy* or *sleasie linen*. This probably had no connection with the modern sense of sleazy (squalid, grimy, dilapidated). According to Eric Partridge, the word was imported into Brtain in the 1950s, from *America*, and combines parts of slimy and greasy.

Singapore   *Gin,* cherry brandy, Cointreau, Benedictine and citrus juices go into the cocktail called a *Singapore sling*. Its invention is attributed to Ngiam Tong Boon, in 1915. At that date he presided over what has often been called the longest bar in the world, that in the Raffles Hotel, *Singapore.*

Sisal   *Sisal* is tough white fibre, from several species of *Agare* and *Fourcroya*, from which strong cordage and string is made. It took its name from the port of *Sisal*, in Yucatan, Mexico, whence this material was exported.

Sitka   The *Sitka spruce* tree (*Picea sitchensis*) takes its name from the small port of *Sitka*, in Alaska, from where it was imported to Britain in 1831.

Sodom   The city of *Sodom* now lies hidden beneath the waters of the Dead Sea. Its wickedness and destruction are described in Genesis 18,19. Centuries later the word *sodomy* was used for 'unnatural sexual intercourse, especially between males'. Hence the allied word *sodomite*, with its shortened version *sod*, and the crude expression '*sod off*'.

Solferino   Exactly like *Magenta*, the Battle of *Solferino* in 1859 gave its name to a bright crimson dye discovered soon afterwards. *Solferino* is about ten miles south of Lake

Garda; there was huge losses in the battle in which, as at *Magenta*, the Austrian forces were defeated by the Franco-Sardinian army.

Soloi A *solecism* is a blunder, a violation of good manners or of good grammar. According to the Greek historian and geographer Strabo (ca 63 BC - ca AD 21), in its literal meaning of 'speaking incorrectly' it refers to the corruption of the *Attic* dialect by Athenian colonists at *Soloi. Soloi* was a port in Cilicia, a district of Southern Anatolia, now in *Turkey.*

Spa Any town which has and has exploited a mineral spring is called a *spa.* All take this appellation from the very first watering place of this kind, the town of *Spa,* in the Ardennes, about 17 miles south-west of Liege. It was famous throughout Europe from the sixteenth century. The pump-room there was built by Peter the Great of *Russia* in 1717. Two centuries later it was the headquarters of the German High Command; Kaiser William II abdicated at *Spa* on 10 November 1918.

Spain *Castles in Spain* are visionary projects, and derive from *Don Quixote* by Cervantes (1547-1616). There are *Spanish* (or sweet) *chestnuts* and *Spanish mahogany*; sycamore trees used to be called *Spanish maples. Spanish fly* is a bright green insect with allegedly aphrodisiac qualities. *Spanish leather* was of high quality. Men's *Spanish breeches* were modish in the seventeenth century. *Spanish kettle-drums* was a popular name for trunk-hose, the ancestor of trousers. The nineteenth century saw many popular *Spanish* items of fashion — men's *Spanish cloaks* (short, with bright linings); *Spanish hats* and *Spanish jackets* for women; and the slashed *Spanish sleeves* which were, like the *hats,* most popular at the time of the Peninsular War.

Spandau In World War II the standard German Army machine gun was a *spandau,* named after the arsenal at *Spandau,* a suburb of West Berlin. After the war, senior Nazi war criminals were imprisoned in *Spandau* gaol, where, for many years now, the lone inmate has been Rudolf Hess.

Sparta *Spartan* means frugal, simple, courageous and terse in speech. The word comes from the city and state of *Sparta,*
76

which was also called Lacedaemon in ancient times. The *Spartans* had a powerful and highly-disciplined army, run on *spartan* lines, and gave the state great influence from the sixth century BC. The place today is marked by the town of *Sparti*, in the Greek province of *Laconia*.

Staffordshire *Staffordshire-ware*, usually shortened to *Staffordshire*, is greatly prized today and much collected. The earthenware and porcelain figures, dogs, miniature cottages and so on were indeed made in the potteries of *Staffordshire*, mainly in the nineteenth century. There is a *Stafford knot* and *Stafford blue* is a cloth, not a colour.

Steenkirk A *steenkirk* was a kind of neckcloth, worn by both sexes, with long laced ends hanging down or twisted together together through a loop or ring. The name derives from the Battle of *Steenkirk*, fought on 3 August 1692, and it is said to allude to the disordered dress of the French, who had been hastily summoned to arms. The battle was fought during the War of the League of Augsburg, between the French and forces organized by William III from *England, Holland* and *Germany*; the French won.

Stellenbosch *Stellenbosch* is the second oldest town in South Africa. It is also a verb. This is because, in the Kaffir Wars in South Africa, incompetent senior British officers were removed from their commands by being posted to the command of the *Stellenbosch* Military District; the place is 30 miles east of Cape Town, and it was supposed that they could do no harm there. The verb was much used, during the Boer Wars, to denote removal from active command in the field. In the early months of World War I, French General officers were similarly removed from active duty by being posted to the command of the *Limoges* Military District; the verb *limoger* was coined to describe this process, the only proper translation being *stellenbosch*.

Stepney Street When motoring was in its pioneering phase, cars were not equipped with spare wheels. Instead they were provided with a *stepney wheel*. This device was an additional all-metal wheel which could be clamped to the spokes of the punctured wheel, so that the car could then limp on to the

77

next garage, where the puncture could be dealt with by experts. The name comes, not from the London Borough of Stepney, but from *Stepney Street*, Llanelli, where *stepney wheels* were first made.

Stoa   The *Stoic* school of philosophy is characterized by the austerity of its ethical doctrines. Founded by Zeno of Citium in *Cyprus* (335-263 BC) it takes its name from the *Stoa Poikile* or Painted Porch, where Zeno taught in *Athens*. *Stoic* or *stoical* has come to mean a show of indifference to pain or hardship.

Stockholm   In the days of wooden ships, many of the products used in ship-building came from Scandinavia, including *Stockholm tar*, made from resinous pine wood.

Strontian   *Strontium* is a silver-white metallic element. The name comes from *Strontian*, on Loch Sunart, Highland Region, where the mineral was first discovered in the lead mines which operated there in the eighteenth century.

Styx   When the cliché '*Stygian* gloom' is used, not all its perpetrators realize that they are referring to the *Styx*, the Underworld river of ancient Greek mythology, over which the souls of the dead were traditionally ferried.

Suffolk   The term *Suffolk School* was invented by picture-dealers as a way to describe assorted nineteenth century followers of the two great Suffolk artists Thomas Gainsborough (1727-88) and John Constable (1776-1837). *Suffolk punches* are a fine breed of thick-set, short-legged draught horses; always chestnuts, they range from light sorrel to dark mahogany in shade. There is a *Suffolk* breed of sheep.

Surrey   Anybody who has seen the musical *Oklahoma!* knows that a *surrey* is a fringe-roofed, four-wheeled, two-seater pleasure carriage. *Surreys* were first introduced to the USA in 1872, and were an adaptation of the *surrey cart*, which indeed originated in the English county of *Surrey*. Some very early motor-cars were made in a similar pattern, and were also called *surreys*.

Swaledale   The *Swaledale* breed of sheep take their name from their native Yorkshire valley.

78

Sweden *Swedes (Brassica campestris)* were once called *Swedish turnips*; they were introduced into Britain, from *Sweden*, in the 1780s. *Suede* was originally, in the mid-nineteenth century, spelt in the French manner (*suède*) and then referred solely to soft kid-skin from *Sweden*, usually used for the manufacture of gloves. Today *suede* has gone on to mean any leather with a nap on the flesh side.

Switzerland Known in the USA as a jelly-roll, a *Swiss roll* is a sponge cake baked in a shallow pan, spread with jam and rolled up while hot. When the tea-shops of J. Lyons abounded, it was they who named and popularized this confection.

Sybaris *Sybaris* was a Greek colony in south *Italy*, founded in 720 BC on the Gulf of Tarentum. It became a prosperous place, and was noted for its luxury. A *sybarite* came to mean, and still means, a person devoted to luxury and pleasure.

Syria One meaning of the word *sorghum* is a genus or group of grasses. The word comes from the Italian *sorgo*, which in turn comes from the Latin *suricum*. This was a corruption of *syricum*, 'of *Syria*'.

T

Tabasco   The very pungent *tabasco sauce* is made from the pulp of the ripe fruit of a variety of pepper: *capiscum annum*. It is named after the *Tabasco* state of Mexico, where this is to be found.

Tamworth   The *Tamworth* breed of pigs, characterized by abundant golden-red hair, originated in and around the *Staffordshire* town of *Tamworth*.

Tangier   *Tangerines (citrus nobilis Tangeriana)* are a small, flattened variety of orange; they came from the Moroccan sea-port of *Tangier*, a British possession from 1661 to 1684. *Tangerines* do not seem to have been known in Britain until the 1840s.

Taranto   A *tarantella* is a rapid, whirling dance, popular in southern *Italy* since the fifteenth century as a remedy for *tarantism*. The latter is an hysterical malady, believed to have been caused by the bite of the *tarantula*, a spider (*Lycosa tarantula*). All three take their names from the southern Italian port of *Taranto*, where the dance, the spiders and the disease flourished.

Tartary   Opinions are divided about the origin of the word *tartan*, except that a Scottish origin seems improbable. One theory is that the word comes from *Tartary*. In medieval times a rich fabric was imported from *Tartary*, and was called *tartarin* or *tarterne*.

Telemark   To the expert on skis, to *telemark* is to swing-turn or stop short. The word comes from the *Telemark* district of *Norway*, where the technique was first devised.

Tennessee   The *Tennessee Walking Horse* is a breed developed in the state of *Tennessee* with the prime purpose of over-seeing plantations; it has a smooth, comfortable and long-lasting gait.

Texas   When a golfer uses a *Texas wedge*, he is in fact using a putter for an approach shot.

Tilbury The old sixpenny piece was sometimes known as a *Tilbury*, as this sum was the fare on the Gravesend to *Tilbury* ferry. However, the carriage called a *tilbury* is a spurious toponym, deriving from the coach-building firm of *Tilbury*, of South Street, Mayfair, *London*, which developed this vehicle about 1820.

Toledo Swords made in the Spanish city of *Toledo* were for centuries thought to be the finest in Europe; they were called *Toledo blades* or *toledos*.

Tolú The highly explosive chemical known as TNT is *tri-nitro-toluene* ($C_6H_2(NO_2)3CH_3$). *Toluene* is so called because it was first obtained, in 1841, by the dry distillation of *tolu balsam*. The latter comes from the bark of the *tolu tree (Myrospermum toluiferum)* which is named after *Tolú* in Colombia.

Torridon *Torridonian sandstone* is a geological formation named after the *Torridon* district of the western *Highlands* of *Scotland*.

Trafalgar The first Lord Nelson (1758-1805) commissioned a combined table and sideboard for his country house at Merton, now absorbed into south *London*, from a firm of patent furniture manufacturers, Morgan and Sanders. After Nelson's death at the great victory off *Cape Trafalgar* on 21 October 1805, the firm marketed the tables as *Trafalgar tables*.

Trappe, Soligny-la- A *Trappist* is a member of a branch of the Cistercian order, established in 1664 at the monastery of *Soligny-la-Trappe* in Normandy. *Trappists* are known for their austerities, which include silence.

Troy To work vigorously or fight valiantly is to do so 'like a *Trojan*'. This is to say, like one of the defenders of *Troy*, as described in Homer's *Iliad*; but the compliment implied by the expression is strange, as the *Trojans* eventually lost to the Greeks. In 1873, Hissarlik in north-west *Turkey* was discovered to have been the site of *Troy*.

81

Troyes The *Troy* system of weights has nothing to do with the ancient world, as the word comes from the French town of *Troyes*, in the *département* of Aube.

Tsentung The word *satin* comes, through the Arabic word *zaiturni*, from the Chinese town of *Tswan-chu-fu* or *Tsentung* where the glossy silk fabric was first made, and whence it was first exported to the West.

Tunbridge Wells Wooden marquetry decoration of many kinds, popular in Regency and Victorian times, is known to furniture experts as *Tunbridge ware.*

Tun-ki *The Widow Twankay* is a pantomime character always played by a man, who acquired her name from *Twankay Tea*, a particular blend of *China* tea, which came from the district of *Tun-ki.*

Turkestan A *turquoise* is a precious stone, which can vary in colour from sky-blue to apple-green. Found in *Persia* the stone got its name from being brought through *Turkestan.*

Turkey *Guinea-fowl* were sometimes called, through extreme geographical ignorance, *turkeys*. Actual *turkeys (meleagris gallopayo)* were found domesticated in Mexico when that country was discovered in 1518. When these began to be brought back to Europe, later in the sixteenth century the mistaken name of *turkey* was even more mistakenly applied to the birds so familiar to us today. *Turkey-cock* has a special meaning: a self-important man. *Turkey carpet, Turkey-corn, turkey-leather, turkish baths, turkish delight,* and *turkish towelling* all come from *Turkey. Turk's head knots* are so-called because of their turban-like appearance. The *Turkey oak (Quercus cerris)* was introduced to Britain in 1735.

Tuxedo The fashion for wearing dinner-jackets, instead of tail-coats for evening wear was started by King Edward VII when Prince of Wales. In 1886 the garment was taken to the USA by Griswold Lorillard. He popularized the dinner-jacket at the *Tuxedo Club*, in *Tuxedo, New York* State; this is why the garment is called a *tuxedo*, or *tux*, in the USA.
82

Tweed (S) The river *Tweed* in southern *Scotland*, famous for its salmon, has given its name to the material, but this was due to an error. The material had been known as *twill*. This was pronounced in *Scotland* as *tweel*, and was also written this way. In 1825 the word *tweel* was misread on an invoice as *tweed*, and the erroneous toponym has been used since that date.

Tyrol The *Tyrolese hat* first became fashionable for women in 1869. A felt hat with a small, flat-topped tapering crown, a narrow brim and a feather cockade, it was made in imitation of men's hats worn in the Austrian *Tyrol*. Versions of this form of headgear are not wholly extinct in *Germany* today. In the 1930s they became fashionable for men, in *Austria* and elsewhere.

U

Ulster   An *ulster* is a long, loose, heavy man's overcoat frequently belted, common enough at the turn of the century but now almost obsolete. The *Ulster overcoat* was introduced by the Belfast firm of J. G. M'Gee & Co in 1867; within a few years, these popular garments had dropped the *overcoat* and became simply *ulsters*. It is not known why they were given the name of the province, rather than the city, of their origin.

Umbria   The colours *burnt umber* and *raw umber* are both made from brown earth, called *terra d'Umbria*, which is to be found in the Italian province of *Umbria*.

Urgendi   The very fine and translucent *muslin* called *organdie* gets its name from the city of *Urgendi*, an ancient centre of weaving, whence this fine fabric originally came. *Urgendi*, now *Urgench*, lies to the south of the Aral Sea, in Uzbekistan, USSR.

Utopia (F)   The principal literary work of Sir Thomas More (1478-1535) was *Utopia*, a speculative essay concerned with the search for a perfect political system, which is said to exist on an imaginary island called *Utopia* (*nowhere* in Greek). The word has been used in this sense since the date of publication, 1516. More wrote in Latin. *Utopia* was first translated into English in 1551, and later into many other languages.

V

Valence *Valences* are used today as hangings for bed-frames; they are also used for the canopies of four-poster beds. There was once a thin woven fabric called *valence*, mentioned by Chaucer. Both the material and the hangings are thought to have taken their name from the town of *Valence* in the *département* of Drôme.

Vau de Vire The twentieth century meaning of *vaudeville* is a variety entertainment. In the eighteenth century it meant popular songs. The word goes back to *chansons vaudevire*, songs from *Vau de Vire*. It is even believed that it was first applied to songs written by a poet called Oliver de Basselin, who died in 1418 and who came from *Vau de Vire*, in Normandy.

Vauxhall In the great days of railways, a Russian party came to *England* to learn about the latest and best in railways. As an example of the latest and the best, they were shown *Vauxhall* station, in *London*. Through faulty interpretation, they were led to believe that the place was the artefact. Accordingly, the Russian for railway-station can be transliterated as *vok'sal*. *Vauxhall* is an odd word, a corruption of *Fox-hall*, which it was called when Pepys was writing his diary in the 1660s.

Venice There were *Venetian hose, Venetian lace* and *Venetian breeches*; also *Venetian bonnets, Venetian cloaks* and *Venetian sleeves. Venetian cloth* has a fine twilled surface. There were *Venetian windows* and *Venetian glass*. The *Venetian School* (of architecture and of painting) flourished in the fifteenth and sixteenth centuries. Most of these are history, but *Venetian blinds* are still much used. The slatted blinds were naturally very useful in the hot *Venetian* summers; they had been copied from the East, and were once called *Persian blinds*.

Vichy *Vichy water*, known in Britain since the 1850s, comes from mineral springs at or near *Vichy*, in *France*. *Vichyssoise* (chilled leek and potato soup) was invented by a chef in the Ritz-Carlton Hotel in *New York* City in 1917, or perhaps earlier. He was called Louis Diat, and he named the delectable soup after his native city of *Vichy*.

Vienna The capital city of the Austro-Hungarian Empire has given its name to two colours: *Vienna green* and the cobalt *Vienna blue*. A *Vienna cross* is an embroidery stitch. The city is also commemorated by various *cakes, bread* and *rolls*. *Vienna rolls* were sometimes called *Kaiser rolls*, from the Emperor Franz-Josef (1830-1916), who reigned from 1848 to 1916.

Virginia The State of *Virginia*, in which the first permanent settlement was at Jamestown in 1607, has given its name to many things found there. Living things include *Virginia bats, Virginia frogs, Virginia nightingales* and *Virginia snap-beetles*. There are *Virginia cedars, Virginia wheat* and *Virginia corn*, but *Virginia tobacco* and *Virginia creeper (Ampelopsis hederacea)* have travelled furthest and widest.

W

Wales   To *welsh* is to swindle by absconding with money laid as a bet or bets. The origin of this expression, which libels a whole nation, is unknown. *Welsh rarebit* was originally *Welsh rabbit*, an eighteenth century mockingly derisive name for toasted cheese. It was altered, perhaps by *Welshmen*, to *Welsh rarebit*, the latter word only being used anywhere in this way. The *Welsh* breed of pigs is an old one, but only became widely known since 1918; *Welsh pigs* are similar to the *Danish Landrace*. The *Welsh*, or *Welsh mountain* breed of pony is similar to the *Highland pony*, but moves faster. There is also a *Welsh mountain* breed of sheep.

Wall Street   *Wall Street*, in down-town *New York* marks the site of the wall built to defend the original Dutch settlement of New Amsterdam. For many years the street, and the area around it, have housed the principal American banks, trust companies, insurance companies and other financial institutions. *Wall Street* has come to mean American finance and financial institutions.

Warri   *Warri* is a West Indian board-game, a complicated form of noughts-and-crosses. Its name comes from the Nigerian port of *Warri*. Similar games are played in many parts of Africa, under different local names and rules.

Waterloo   To meet one's *Waterloo* is to succumb to eventual defeat, as Napoleon did to the forces under the command of the first Duke of Wellington on 18 June 1815. The well-preserved battlefield, near *Brussels*, is called *Waterloo* from the name of the village where Wellington had spent the previous night.

Wessex   The hardy and prolific *Wessex saddleback* breed of pigs originated in Dorset. The Saxon Kingdom of *Wessex* stretched from Cornwall to Sussex, and north to Hereford; it disappeared after the Norman Conquest.

Whitechapel   The *London* borough of *Whitechapel* gave its name to a light two-wheeled spring cart, the *Whitechapel cart*. A *Whitechapel shave* is achieved by application of whitening to the jaw with the hand. *Whitechapel play*, in whist, is to lead out the aces, and kings, a technique also known as 'kitchen-whist'. But, also in whist, a *whitechapel* is a lead of a 'singleton' with a view to future trumping.

Whitehall The name of the street, *Whitehall*, commemorates the old *Whitehall Palace*, once the London residence of Archbishops of *York*, and known as York Place, but taken from Cardinal Wolsey (1473-1530) by Henry VIII, who extended it and renamed it *Whitehall Palace*. It was both a royal residence and the sea of government and was largely destroyed by fire in 1698. Today only a minority of Government Ministries is actually in *Whitehall*, but the word is used to describe the Government as a whole. '*Whitehall* sources' can mean anything from a junior official to the Prime Minister speaking off the record.

White House, The Journalists have given *The White House*, in Pennsylvania Avenue, Washington DC, a voice of its own, like any other government headquarters. '*White House*' opinion is often quoted and referred to. Unlike many such buildings, *The White House* was purpose-built, from 1792 to 1800 as the official residence of the President of the United States. It was built of grey limestone, and painted white at a later date. It was partly destroyed by British troops in 1814 and rebuilt.

Wilton *Wilton* in Wiltshire has been celebrated for the manufacture of carpets since the reign of Elizabeth I. Today a *Wilton* carpet may not necessarily have been made there, but it ought to mean that it is made by the method developed at the *Wilton* Royal Carpet Factory (with which the *Axminster* factory merged early in the nineteenth century).

Winchester (S) The famous Winchester rifle is not a toponym, but is named after Oliver F. Winchester (1810-1880), an American manufacturer of guns and ammunition.

Windsor The supremely comfortable *Windsor chair* was first made in the Royal Borough of *Windsor*. With separated legs, arms and backs, tapered joints and a saddle-seat, they have been popular since the early eighteenth century; they were much used in coffee-houses where their long-lasting qualities were valued. *Windsor bricks*, a fire-resisting type, were formerly made in the near-by village of Hedgerley. *Windsor soap* is brown and scented. *Windsor uniform* is formal evening wear worn at *Windsor* by male members of the Royal Family and other privileged persons; introduced by George III it is blue, with red cuffs and collars.

Worcester *Worcester porcelain* was made at a factory established in 1751, originally at *Bristol*, by Benjamin Lund and William Miller. This became the most productive porcelain factory in England. *Worcestershire sauce*, a proprietary name, is so called because the recipe came from an old *Worcestershire* family, according to the labels on the bottles.

Worstead *Worsted*, usually spelt thus, is defined as 'woollen fabric made from well twisted yarn spun of long-staple wool combed to lay the fibres parallel'. It takes its name from the Norfolk village of *Worstead*, where Flemish weavers established themselves as early as the twelfth century.

Wycombe The furniture-making centre of *High Wycombe*, in Buckinghamshire has given its name to two styles of plain wooden chair: *White Wycombe* and *Kitchen Wycombe*.

Y

Yorkshire A perfect *yorker*, in cricket, is a ball which pitches with great precision immediately under the bottom of the bat: a hard, fast and straight delivery, much prized by bowlers. The name comes from the perennial skill and enthusiasm of cricketers from *Yorkshire*. *Yorkshire pudding* (baked batter) eaten with, or sometimes before, roast beef is a classic English dish. The very important Large White breed of pigs should properly be called by their original name of *Large White Yorkshire*.

Index

Cognac 3
coins 32, 36, 65, 71, 81
Coldstream, Sir William 31
collars
    Astrakhan 4
    Eton 31
Colling brothers 29
colours
    Cambridge blue 17
    gamboge 17
    Lovat green 49
    Oxford blue 61
    Prussian blue 66
    Siena 74
    umber 84
    Vienna blue 86
    Vienna green 86
comfort, Dutch 38
condoms 33
Condon, Eddie 21
conga 23
Constable, John 8, 78
contraceptives 33, 38
cooker, Benghazi 10
copper 25
    verdigris on 36
cord, Bedford 9
cordage making in *Bridport* 14
corduroy 30
cordwain 24
corn
    Turkey- 82
    Virginia 86
corn-row hair-style 23
Cotman, John Sell 59
cotton cloth
    calico 17
    Cretonne 25
    denim 58
    dungaree 28
    nankeen 57
courage, Dutch 38
covered wagon 23
coverlets, *Afghan* 2
Craig, Elijah 13
cranes, known as *scotchmen* 72
cravats 4, 25
Creed, Nicene 58
creeper, Virginia 86
crepe, Norwich 59
crepe de chine 21
Crete, labyrinth in 45
cricket
    French 33
    Nottingham forward cut 59
    yorker 90
94

Crimean War 6
criminal record 57
Crome, John 59
crosses, Maltese 52
cross-stitch *see* embroidery
crows, Norway 59
cudgels 65, 74
cuffs, French 33
currants 24
cutlery cleaning, *Bristol brick*
    for 14
cypress trees 25

Daedalus 45
daggers 9, 64
daisy, Paris 62
damask, Norwich 59
damson 26
dances
    Boston two-step and *waltz*
        13
    Charleston 20
    Cheshire round 20
    conga 23
    Highland fling 38
    mazurka 34
    pavan 62
    polka 65
    Polonaise 65
    schottische 72
    tarantella 80
Darley Arab 3
de Worde, Wynkyn 40
debunk 16
Defoe, Daniel 4
degrees, Lambeth 45
denim 58
desk, *Derbyshire* 27
desk-tables, *Carlton House* 18
diamonds 43
Diat, Louis 85
dinner-jackets 82
Disraeli, Benjamin 6
divan 61
dogs
    Aberdeen terriers 1, 72
    Afghan hounds 2
    Blenheim terriers 13
    Boston terriers 13
    Dalmatian 26
    Maltese 52
    Norfolk spaniels 58
    Norfolk terriers 58
    Norwich terriers 58, 59
    Pekingese 9
dollars 71

frogs, *Virginia* 86
fruit mixture 50
Fry, Roger 12
furniture
    Canterbury 18
    Portuguese legs 66
    Wycombe 89
furniture, oak 1
fustian 30

Gainsborough, Thomas 78
gallop, Canterbury 18
gamboge 17
games
    Badminton 6
    boston 13
    chevy 21
    Newmarket 57
    Olympic Games 60
    Rubicon bezique 69
    Russian bagatelle 69
    Russian banker 69
    Warri 87
    whist 87
Garcinia tree 17
gauze 34
gems 1
    turquoise 82
German gown 15
gin, Plymouth 65
gin-and-bitters 2
gipsies 13, 30
girdles, Culross 25
glass, Venetian 85
Gloire de Dijon 27
Gloria Mundi, New York 58
gloves, Berlin 10
goats, Angora 2
Godolphin Barb 3
goitre 27
golf
    approach shot 56
    Schenectady putter 72
    Texas wedge 80
'gone for a burton' 16
government headquarters
    British 28
    Russian 44
    United States 88
gown, Brunswick 15
Grant, Duncan 12, 49
grass
    Kentucky blue 43
    Rhode Island bent 68
    sorghum 79
greatcoats, Polish 65

96

griddles 25
guinea-fowl 82
Gulliver's travels 47
gum-resin, yellow pigment
    from 17
guns
    Bren 14
    naval 19
    Oerlikon 60
    pistols 64

hack-work, literary 36
haddock, Finnan 32
hair-oil, *Macassar* 50
hair-styles
    Boston slashback 13
    congo 23
    Eton crops 31
    Guinea 36
hallmarks 35
ham, *Parma* 63
Hamlet 3
hand-gallop 18
hand-grenades, known as 'pine-
    apples' 21
handkerchiefs
    Barcelona 8
    cambric for 17
hangings 3
Harvard University 28
hats
    Astrakhan 4
    Bermuda 10
    bretons 14
    Caudebec 19
    Danish cocks 26
    Derby 27
    Egham Staines and Windsor
        30
    fez 32
    Henley boaters 37
    homburg 38
    Leghorn 46
    milliners 55
    Monmouth caps 55
    Oatland village 60
    Panama 62
    Scarborough 72
    Spanish 76
    Tyrolese 83
    Venetian bonnets 85
Hawkins, Anthony Hope 69
hawthorn 35
heels, French 33
heels, Italian 40
helmets, *balaclavas* 6